AMERICAN CLASSICS
OF THE AIR

AMERICAN CLASSICS
OF THE AIR

Commercial and Private Aeroplanes from the 1920s to the 1960s

Geoff Jones & Chuck Stewart

MBI Publishing Company

Acknowledgments

Geoff Jones and Chuck Stewart would like to thank the hundreds of owners and pilots whose cooperation over the past few years has helped in the assembly of the photographs featured in this book. Not only are the photos an indication of the skill of the owner and restorer, but also of the pilots' skill in flying them for the authors' cameras. No one is singled out, but a big 'THANK YOU!' to all who helped to make this book possible and for enriching the world of aviation for present and future generations.

This edition first published in 2000 by MBI Publishing Company, 729 Prospect Avenue, PO Box 1, Osceola, WI 54020-0001 USA.

Previously published by Airlife Publishing Ltd, Shrewsbury, England.

MBI Publishing Company books are also available at discounts in bulk quantity for industrial or sales-promotional use. For details write to Special Sales Manager at Motorbooks International Wholesalers & Distributors, 729 Prospect Avenue, PO Box 1, Osceola, WI 54020-0001 USA.

Library of Congress Cataloging-in-Publication Data available

ISBN 0-7603-0901-9

Printed in Hong Kong

Contents

Introduction

Each of the two major world wars spawned an unprecedented rush in the development of technology. Nowhere has this been better illustrated than in the field of aviation. Whilst the aircraft described in words and pictures in this book are all civilian, their existence owes much to the aeronautical designers and manufacturers who reached their zenith during wartime and then had to adapt to the more fickle civilian market.

Our aeronautical adventure in *American Classics of the Air* starts in the 1920s and proceeds in subsequent decades to the 1960s. When companies such as Cessna started manufacturing 150s and 172s in the 1950s and '60s, it was hard to conceive that such aircraft would eventually acquire 'classic' status in years to come. History has overtaken events and many of these '50s and '60s types are now highly sought after. They have become rapidly appreciating aeronautical assets.

In 30 or 40 years, we may find ourselves refurbishing 1999-vintage New Piper Malibu Meridians with what will then be their archaic digital instrumentation and museum-piece global positioning systems. *Tempus fugit*, particularly in aviation!

All of the aircraft featured in these pages are currently or have recently been in airworthy condition, and as the book's title suggests, have been photographed in their element – the air and mostly air-to-air. Sadly, one or two have crashed since these photos were taken. Being a book about American aircraft, most of the photography was done in the U.S., the bulk of it under sunny California skies. However, the U.S. does not have an exclusive on American Classic aircraft and several of the featured aircraft are European-based.

There is no particular qualification for any of the aircraft featured other than being a preserved, flying example of an aircraft considered representative of a particular era. Many of the aircraft have undergone lengthy rebuilds and are a credit to their restorers, owners and pilots. Their value in terms of dollars or pounds is often inestimable. Owners lavish considerable TLC on these aircraft, fly them only during good weather and frequently receive awards at the fly-ins and airshows they attend.

The question of selling them, whilst it may be broached, is not usually discussed. These airlpanes are, after all, often one of the family, a 'pet' or more often, a 'mistress'. Most of the more popular models of these aircraft also have 'type clubs' so that owners and enthusiasts have a forum for support and exchange of information. All the currently known type clubs and societies for aircraft featured in this book are detailed in the Appendix to enable readers to contact fellow enthusiasts of these classic American aircraft.

Where can you see some of these classics at close quarters? There are numerous events throughout North America and the rest of the world. The Experimental Aircraft Association's regional fly-ins in the U.S. are a good place to start. Here, classics are often gathered in the hundreds and visitors can get up-close access to a variety of aircraft.

The EAA Sun 'n Fun Fly-In is held in Lakeland, Florida each April; the Northwest Regional Fly-In at Arlington, Washington is held in July; the Golden West Regional Fly-In is in Atwater, California in September; and the Copperstate Fly-In is held in Mesa, Arizona each October. 'The world's largest airshow', bar none, takes place in Oshkosh, Wisconsin the last week of July and into the first week of August.

But these big shows aren't everyone's cup of tea. If you want to look and chat about antique and classic aircraft from dawn till dusk, you might find smaller events such as the Watsonville, California Fly-In in late May, the National Biplane Association Fly-In at Bartlesville, Oklahoma in early June, or the Antique Aircraft Association Fly-In at Blakesburg, Iowa in May more convivial.

The classic aircraft movement is burgeoning in Europe as well. The Popular Flying Association's annual rally at Cranfield, Bedfordshire, England normally the first weekend in July (but the last weekend in June in 2000) is the biggest such event outside North America and attracts many American-built antiques and classics. The 'Calendar' pages of most aviation magazines are crammed with summertime events for pilots and the public; make a resolution to visit one and see some of America's aviation history in the air.

Biplanes with open cockpits and taildragger undercarriage were the norm amongst U.S. manufacturers of the early 1920s. Manufacturing costs were low and two wings gave better lift with the relatively heavy engines of the day. After both world wars, aircraft were almost 'ten-a-penny' and airfields were cluttered with surplus ex-military types. Many former servicemen with flying experience but no jobs tried their luck purchasing some of these aircraft and using them for a variety of commercial tasks, including stunt flying.

One type more than any other got private civilian flying established in the U.S. after WW I: the Curtiss JN-4D 'Jenny'. From 1916 on, the Curtiss company built more than 10,900 Jennies, including 2,900 in Canada. Some 6,163 were procured by the U.S. Air Service in 1917-18 and several thousand were sold surplus in the early 1920s. Incredibly, a handful remain airworthy in the U.S. today, more than 80 years on.

In the 1920s, America was a vast country, mainly the province of the railroad if people wanted to travel any distance. When the first pioneers started thinking about establishing air services, it wasn't to carry passengers but mail. In fact, several of today's major U.S. airlines, including Northwest and American Air Lines, got their starts with the U.S. Mail contracts granted under the 1925 Kelly Air Mail Act. Their first aircraft were basic, open-cockpit biplanes: flying simply for fun or for sport was almost non-existent.

Civil aviation's transition from a 'backyard' aircraft manufacturing industry to what would now be recognized as commercial manufacturing concerns got going in the mid-1920s. In response to this upsurge of aircraft manufacturing, the U.S. Department of Commerce decided it should introduce a means of approving the aircraft that were now being sold. Their solution was to give each commercially designed and built civil aircraft an 'Approved Type Certificate'. This effectively marked the birth of the commercial aircraft industry in the U.S.

Approved Type Certificate No.1, issued in March 1927, was to the little-known Buhl-Verville J4 Airster CA-3. As an illustration of the burgeoning U.S. aircraft industry, the Commerce Dept. certificated some 284 different types over the next three years, saturating the relatively small market. In 1927, many other types were certificated, mostly biplanes, many of them with the readily available Curtiss OX-5 radial engine and all of them taildraggers. One or two monoplane designs appeared, the imported Fokker Universal being the first, followed by the Fairchild FC-2, the first such indigenously designed and built American aircraft.

Names that appeared in these early annals of the Commerce Department's certification process were Boeing, with its Model 40A; Douglas, with its Model's O-2, M-2 and M-4; and Waco, with its Model 9 – all of which were certificated in June and July 1927. Other early famous names were the Stinson Detroiter and the Pitcairn Mailwing PA-5, both in November 1927, and the Kreider-Reisner Challenger C-2 in December 1927. Several of these early certificated types are featured in this book.

Some of the other famous names of these formative years were Bellanca, Cessna, Command-Aire, Consolidated, Curtiss, Ford, Laird, Lincoln, Lockheed, Monocoupe, Ryan, Sikorsky, Spartan, Stearman and Travel Air – a veritable microcosm of the emerging commercial U.S. aviation industry.

Of these, the Travel Air company was particularly prolific with its 2000, 3000, 4000, 8000 and 9000 models, all certificated in 1928, all biplanes and all designed by the partnership of Walter Beech and Clyde Cessna. Their adaptability to a variety of tasks, from pilot training to mail carriage and bush flying, meant they were built in larger numbers than any other contemporary aircraft. That adaptability is why so many of them survive today – large numbers were used for decades as cropdusters. That is where the beautiful Travel Air featured in this book came from.

It is also prudent to note the two names that were instrumental in Travel Air: Beech and Cessna. The companies they subsequently founded probably did more for the commercial and general aviation industry in the U.S. than any others. There are plenty of examples of both Cessnas and Beechcrafts in this book.

A type that was built in Cleveland between 1929 and '32 has endured more than any other; former Waco employee Charles Meyers' Great Lakes biplane. With several revivals by various entrepreneurs, with various design modifications and shifts of location, the Great Lakes biplane was still being built in limited numbers well into the 1980s.

The Weaver Aircraft Company, thus the acronym 'WACO', is in a similar niche position, with the Lansing, Michigan-based Classic Aircraft Corp., still building small numbers of a much updated version of the 1934 Waco YMF-5 in 1999. The most recent classic types to be revived are the Luscombe 8 Silvaire, now being manufactured by Renaissance Aircraft of Monkton, Maryland and the Monocoupe 110 Special manufactured by Aviat Aircraft of Afron, Wyoming. Powered by a Lycoming O-320 engine, the 'new' Luscombes sell for just under $80,000 and a 200-hp Textron Lycoming AE10-360 in the case of the Monocoupe. Observers should relish the opportunity to look at and fly such aircraft even though they are not original 1930's aircraft.

Another major contribution to the development of the American aviation industry was the so-called Golden Age of air racing, symbolized for so many by Jimmy Doolittle's red and white, barrel-shaped Gee Bee R-2 racer. Several races had been held before and after WW I, but the real catalyst was the inauguration in 1923 of the Pulitzer Trophy Race, followed in 1924 by the National Air Races. Almost entirely the province of military planes and pilots, the 1924 Nationals at Dayton, Ohio were the first races specifically for civilian aircraft. This race was then held annually and supplemented in 1930 by the Thompson Trophy Race, held annually until 1939.

The National and Thompson races did more than anything else to introduce the American public to aviation and spur the development of aircraft and engines. Thousands of people came to these spectacles to see such futuristic aircraft as the Laird 'Speedwing' flown by Bill Ong in 1931 and the Brown B-2 Special *Miss Los Angeles* flown by Roy Minor and McKeen in 1936. Photos of both these types are featured in this book, albeit the B-2 is a replica built in the 1980s by Bill Turner's Repeat Aircraft Co. in Rubidoux, California.

Despite the Great Depression and the number of aircraft manufacturers trying to muscle in on a limited market, new types and new design innovations kept appearing. Wacos were very much the aircraft of the time. Despite sticking resolutely to the biplane formula, Waco did at least concede to enclosed cockpits, such as on its 1931 Model QDC.

Another superb design that also featured an enclosed cockpit in a biplane configuration was the Beech 17 'Staggerwing', first flown in 1932 and produced well into the 1940s. Not only were its reverse-stagger wings innovative, it also featured a retractable undercarriage, almost the first time this had been available on a civilian aircraft. Beech also introduced their twin-engine, twin-tail Beech 18 in January 1937, another design that was to set many trends in civil aviation.

In the spring of 1933 Don A. Luscombe left the Monocoupe Company to establish his own company at Kansas City. A whole string of Luscombe designs followed, the 8C Silvaire being the most successful, with more than 6,000 built and production continuing until 1961. Luscombes are also featured in this book.

Another big name in U.S. civil aviation is Piper. Their first commercial product was the Piper J-3 Cub in 1937, evolved from the Taylor E-2 Cub of 1930. The J-3 and its derivatives are arguably the best known, most popular group of light aircraft ever, a popularity enhanced by the Cub's sterling military service during WW II.

Aeronca (the Aeronautical Corporation of America) paralleled Piper and its Cub, introducing its Model C-2 at the Los Angeles Air Races in 1929. The C-3 was a popular lightplane in the 1930s and its Model LC of 1935 was a radical low-wing monoplane, only one of which remains flying today and is included in this book. Like the Cub, their Aeronca 65 series stood the company in good stead as training and liaison aircraft at the outset of WW II.

Cessna, meanwhile, was improving its designs, first with the high-wing C-34 in 1934 and then the C-145 and C-165 Airmaster. Their sprung undercarriage and strutless wings gave them good looks and good performance, helping put Cessna back in the private civil aeroplane business in 1934 after the company almost disappeared from existence. Cessna, like Beech, also produced a twin-engine design: the T-50, first flown in 1939 and variously known as the Bobcat, Crane and Bamboo Bomber. It was built by the thousands largely as a result of its adoption during the war by the military as the AT-8, AT-17 and UC-78.

World War Two contributed to the post-war civil aviation scene more significantly than any other event in the history of U.S. civil aviation. Aircraft production had increased immensely as part of the war effort and as the major manufacturers concentrated on the hardware of war – the fighters and bombers – the now-established civil aircraft manufacturers built thousands of smaller aircraft: trainers, liaison aircraft, spotters, utility types, etc.

But when the war ended and civil flying got going again, production was severely curtailed and the bottom fell out of the civilian light aircraft market. That was not to say that the manufacturers predicted such a downturn. In fact, they had hoped that the thousands of returning airmen would want to buy and fly their own aircraft. Not so! A few did, but the thousands of war-surplus Cubs, Aeroncas, Luscombes, Stearmans, etc. were much more affordable.

One of the big benefits of the war was that the aviation industry learned how to build and manufacture all-metal aircraft. The pre-war American preference had been for a welded steel-tube fuselage frame covered by fabric and wood- or metal-framed wings, again fabric-covered. The durability of these structures was not great.

North American, for instance, had been building its all-metal P-51 Mustang at their Inglewood, California plant. To take up the slack as Mustang production was reduced, NAA decided to build personal aeroplanes for the anticipated surge in the market. By May of 1946, its year-old L-143 project, was redesignated the NA-143 and named the Navion. It was an all-metal, low-wing four-seater monoplane powered by a 185-hp engine intended for the civilian market but manufactured in almost military style. A thousand Navions were built by June 1947, but the market was saturated.

Competing against Cessna's Model 120s and 140s, Piper had to cut its prices and specifications. The extremely basic PA-15 Vagabond resulted. Beech also went the route of the metal, low-wing retractable with the Bonanza, which was characterized by its unique V tail. One of the most successful light aircraft ever built, it entered production in 1947 and in updated versions, has remained in continuous production ever since.

Cessna's somewhat less sleek but certainly classy competition was the Cessna 190 and 195, a pair of strutless high-wing taildraggers descended from the pre-war Model 165 Airmaster. The post-war general aviation slump was perhaps best illustrated by Piper, which delivered 7,817 aircraft in 1946 alone but by 1951 had cut its annual production to just over 1,000 aircraft.

Just as open cockpits and biplanes were eclipsed by enclosed cockpits and monoplanes in the 1930s, so in the 1950s was the conventional taildragger superseded by tricycle gear. Designs featuring tricycle gear had been built before the war, the Waco AVN-8 of 1938 was something of a novelty, particularly as it was a biplane.

The 1937 Ercoupe was one of the most popular early tri-gear light aircraft, with more than 5,500 built since 1946. In the 1950s, the two-seat market was dominated by two manufacturers: Cessna and Piper. Piper was first off the mark with a tri-gear version of the PA-20 Pacer in 1951: the PA-22 Tri-Pacer of relatively outmoded rag-and-tube construction. Cessna's first tri-gear offering, the Model 150, was developed from the earlier taildragger Model 140, but was all-metal and first flew in September 1957.

History has now shown that production of Cessna's 150 and its many tri-gear, high-wing, strut-braced singles has far outstripped those of Piper. Piper abandoned the high wing for the low wing of its famous John Thorpe-designed PA-28 Cherokee.

According to the EAA, an Antique aeroplane is one built prior to 1946, a Classic between 1946 and 1955, and a Contemporary between 1956 and 1960. Thus, this book includes aircraft of the antique, classic and contemporary eras under the generic 'Classic' category. At any rate, the coverage in this book ends with aircraft built in 1969.

American Classics of the Air is necessarily just a scratch on the surface of the civil general aviation industry in America from the early 1920s to the 1960s. The selection of aircraft types is admittedly somewhat hit-and-miss, but we have tried to include the most important and representative types, along with a few more esoteric and unusual types, such as the Fleetwing Seabird and Howard 500, for example.

Most importantly, all of the aircraft featured here are flyers, which means they are still doing what they were designed to do so many years before. In the air is where these winged beauties belong and where they are shown off to best advantage. We hope that, as you thumb the pages of this book, you will agree.

Kreider-Reisner KR.31 Challenger (1928)

NC7780 was restored and flown by Bill Watson of Collingsville (near Tulsa), Oklahoma and photographed at the National Biplane Association Fly-In, Bartlesville, Oklahoma in June 1995. Tragically, NC7780 was destroyed, killing Watson and two others in a fatal accident at Bartlesville in 1996.

Approximately 200 KR.31s were built in Hagerstown, Maryland between 1928 and 1930, the type being superceded by the KR.34. The company was named after Amos Kreider and Lewis Reisner, who owned the Waco dealership for Maryland and Pennsylvania.

It is no surprise, therefore, that the biplane, open-cockpit, three-seat KR.31 (also called the C-3) was a development of the type originally known as the C-2, which was a copy, with improved performance, of the Waco 9. 'Challenger' was a generic name adopted for several of the KR models because of the company's success in air races and air tours with aircraft flown by Kreider and Ted Kenyon.

A variety of engines were used, the most common being the OX-5, but a few Kinner-, Comet- and Warner-powered variants were also built. The OX-5 variants had the radiator mounted on top of the cowling, a distinguishing feature that did little to enhance forward visibility. A new KR.31 cost around $5,000 in 1929.

In 1929, Fairchild took over the assets of the Kreider-Reisner Co. and the next KR type, the C-4 Challenger, became known as the Fairchild KR.34.

Open cockpit delight, Bill Watson flying his Kreider-Reisner KR.31 Challenger (GPJ).

The water cooled OX-5 engine of the KR.31 required this characteristic radiator, a considerable hindrance to the forward view (GPJ).

Pilot behind and room for two passengers in front in the KR.31 (GPJ).

Fairchild 71 (1929)

This 1929 Fairchild 71 is owned by Tom Dixon of Lodi, California, who first saw the plane in the February 1970 issue of *Sport Flying* magazine. Fascinated with the plane, Dixon made it his business to meet the man who restored it, Gaylord E. Moxon, at the Merced Antique Fly-In later that summer.

From then on, he was determined to own a Fairchild 71. But it wasn't until 1993 that he finally bought N2K from Moxon. Up until an engine failure forced him to put down in an Iowa cornfield in 1997, Dixon flew the Fairchild on weekend jaunts to airshows all over the state. These photographs were taken at the Watsonville West Coast Antique Fly-In in May 1996.

N2K was manufactured by Fairchild in Farmingdale, Long Island, New York in July 1929 and remained registered to Fairchild until it was sold to American Airways in August 1932. After three years with American, it passed through several private owners in quick succession, then was acquired by Fairchild Aerial Surveys in 1935.

Based at Burbank, California, the plane was used as a camera ship for high-altitude photo-mapping assignments across the Western U.S. for more than 20 years. There are rumors that it was used on overseas missions, but Dixon can't verify it because the earliest logbooks he has are from 1948.

In 1955, Fairchild Aerial Surveys sold N2K, along with another Fairchild 71 and an FC-2W2, to Charlie Jensen, a well-known cropduster from Sacramento, Calif. Jensen eventually sold the two Model 71s and N2K wound up in Texas smuggling textiles across the border from Mexico.

In 1963, it was bought by G.E. Moxon and restored. All of the sheet metal was formed from scratch, all of the wood was replaced on the fuselage and the entire airframe recovered and painted in original colours. The interior was redone in a passenger configuration, which entailed the construction of six wicker seats. When the restoration was completed in 1969, N2K emerged in like-new condition.

Although Moxon took it to many fly-ins around the country and won numerous awards, he didn't fly it much after 1978. In fact, it sat in a hangar at Corona Airport, California, with its wings folded for 15 years, not flying until it was forced to escape rising water during a flood in 1982.

When the airport flooded again in 1992, the Fairchild was towed to high ground on the airport and shortly thereafter, purchased by Dixon.

'The Fairchild has exceptional handling qualities in the air', Dixon says. 'It's stable yet responsive: a real pleasure to fly'.

The stable, sturdy Fairchild 71 found its niche as a sightseeing and aerial photo platform. Only a handful survive today, more in museums than on active flightlines (CRS).

N2K's owner, Tom Dixon, cruising Northern California's Pacific coastline at a leisurely 95 mph behind a 450-hp Pratt & Whitney Wasp Junior engine (CRS).

Opposite:
(Top) Often likened to a flying bus, the Fairchild 71 has a useful load of 2,750 pounds and easily carries a pilot and six passengers in its creaky wicker seats (CRS).

(Bottom) Remove a few bolts and the Fairchild 71's wings fold straight back for easy towing or hangar storage (CRS).

Laird LC-RW300 'Speedwing' (1929)

NC4442 is owned by Federal Express MD-11 captain Jim Rollison of Vacaville, California and believed to be the only one of six built that is still flying.

Manufacture of this particular aircraft was begun but never completed at the E.M. Laird Airplane Co. in Chicago, Illinois in 1929-30, just as the stock market crash cut the customer base for Speedwings (considered an expensive luxury at the time, priced between $11,500 and $14,250) to a precious few who could afford them.

The partially complete aircraft was acquired by Rollison's father in 1960 after being moved from warehouse to warehouse in a nomadic existence. His ambition to rebuild the last of the line to airworthy condition never materialised and in 1990 he sold the Laird to his son, Jim Jr.

Realising the enormity of the rebuilding task, Jim Jr. decided to contract out the restoration to Dan Murray in Santa Paula, California. In 1993, exactly 13 months to the day after the parts were delivered to Murray, the Laird was rolled out and flown for the very first time.

Laird Specials quickly acquired notoriety in the 1920s, largely a result of the exploits of air race and pioneer pilot, Charles 'Speed' Holman. The first Laird LC-R300, a three-seat, open-cockpit biplane (the front cockpit is faired over on Rollison's aircraft) fitted with a 300-hp Wright J6 radial engine. The later versions were custom-built under 'Matty' Laird's supervision.

This restored aircaft has a 450-hp Pratt & Whitney R-985, which makes it a really manoeuverable and powerful aircraft with a cruise speed of 170 mph, a 20-gallon-per-hour fuel burn and a 3.2 hours endurance. It's no lightweight either, with an empty weight of 1,500 pounds and gross weight of 2,500 lbs. As one would expect from an aircraft honed to flying perfection, it is a graceful and superbly agile aerobatic performer.

This model was the last of the line for Lairds. By 1935, the Chicago factory had been vacated to make way for manufacture of Benny Howard's new DGA monoplanes. This unique aircraft is valued at $395,000 by its owner.

Beautiful restoration of the Laird 'Speedwing' by Dan Murray at Santa Paula (GPJ).

Above: The Laird Company were synonymous with high quality and high performance aircraft (GPJ).

'Superbly manoeuvrable, agile and a joy to fly' says owner Jim Rollison of his Laird (GPJ).

Valued at $395,000, this 1929/30 Laird 'Speedwing' is unique (GPJ).

Travel Air 4000 (1929)

Based at Frazier Lake, California, NC8877 was restored over a 10-year period by Lonnie and Josie Autry and flown for these photos at the June 1997 Merced Pilots Association Antique Airplane Fly-In by Doug Moreland.

The plane appears in the colours of Pacific Air Transport, a precursor to United Air Lines, that flew the C.A.M.8 air mail route. Although it is claimed that this aircraft flew with PAT, PAT sold out to Boeing Air Transport in April 1929 and this particular aircraft wasn't assigned a registration until at least April 1929. It is therefore unlikely that, despite the owners claims, the aircraft is an ex-PAT mail-hauler. Regardless, it has been restored to superb condition and was awarded the top prizes at both big Californian antique aircraft fly-ins in 1997: Merced and Watsonville.

Travel Air Inc. was formed in Wichita, Kansas by Walter Innes Jr., Lloyd Stearman, Walter Beech and Clyde V. Cessna in February 1925. Having built 65 assorted aircraft in 1925 and '26, including the Travel Air 1000, their Travel Air 2000, powered by the venerable OX-5 engine, was the design that catapulted the company from a smalltime aircraft builder to a major manufacturer.

Approximately 600 Model 2000s were built, the design being followed by the 3000 and the 4000 (also known as the J5 Travel Air because of its engine, the 220-hp Wright J5) in 1926.

Superb restoration by Lonnie and Josie Autry of this 1929 Travel Air 4000 (GPJ).

Except for the engine, it was almost identical to the 2000; although several of the 600 built were fitted with different engines during production.

The Travel Air 4000 was used extensively for pilot training and as an executive transport, particularly by the Phillips Petroleum Co. They were also used to carry mail as part of the Contract Air Mail routes awarded following the 1925 Kelly Act. C.A.M.8, which ran from Los Angeles to Seattle, with stops in San Francisco and Portland, was awarded to Oregon-based bus operator Vern Gorst in January 1926. With contract in hand, he formed Pacific Air Transport and purchased a handful of Travel Airs.

NC8877 was purchased by three brothers and operated from Hanford, California between 1930-34 before moving to an agricultural operator who used it for rice-seeding and cropdusting until 1961. It was sold in unairworthy condition to Ray Stephens in 1968, who in turn sold it to Autry in 1986.

The Autrys finished their Travel Air 4000 in the colours of Pacific Air Transport (GPJ).

Travel Airs were built in large numbers in the 1920s and '30s – over 50 survive today (GPJ).

Flying near its Frazier Lake, California base, the 1929 Travel Air 4000 (GPJ).

Fairchild (Kreider-Reisner) KR.21 (1930)

NC236V, NC107M and NC209V are owned by Dan Reid, Robin Reid and Rafael 'Curly' and Dorene Medina, respectively. The first two are based at Reid-Hillview airport near San Jose, California, the third at Redding, California.

NC236V was sold new in July 1930 and flown to California by Cecil Reid and Robert 'Pop' Reid in 1932. It has been owned by the Reid family ever since. Dan Reid, its owner, is Cecil's grandson. NC107M was purchased by Robin Reid's father Bobby in the 1950s and has been in the family ever since.

'Curly' Medina has owned NC209V for almost 40 years and is a close friend of the Reid family. These three KR.21s are believed to be the only three airworthy examples remaining out of a total of 48 built between 1929 and 1931.

With the sales successes in 1929 of other two-seat biplanes, particularly the Great Lakes 2-T-1 and Waco 'Taperwing', Kreider-Reisner's Fred Seiler designed the high-performance two-seat C-6 Sport Trainer to compete. A 100-hp Kinner K5 radial was installed for the 48 aircraft built, although five additional aircraft were powered by

various sizes of inline Ranger engines.

The Kreider-Reisner Co. became a susidiary of Fairchild in 1929, so the aircraft was designated the Fairchild KR-21A. Developed from this in 1930 was the KR.21B, with a more powerful 125-hp Kinner B5 engine and considerably more attention to stream-lining, its faired wing struts and wheelpants being most noticeable. Only three KR.21Bs were built and two KR.21As modified.

The KR.21A's aerobatic ability is demonstrated today by Robin Reid, who performs an aerobatic routine at airshows in NC107M.

Kinner K5 radial engines distinguish this trio of KR.21s (GPJ).

Opposite above: Robin Reid, Dan Reid and 'Curly' Medina (L. to R.) flying their KR.21s over rich agricultural land in central California (GPJ).

Unique formation at the time of, what are believed to be, the only three airworthy KR.21s (GPJ).

Opposite below: Robin Reid's KR.21 NC107M has performed at Californian air shows since 1998 (GPJ).

Great Lakes 2-T-1 Biplane (1930)

Blue-and-white N844K is owned by Bill Ewertz and yellow-and-white N847K is owned by his wife Jan; both aircraft were based at Gnoss Field in Schellville, north of San Francisco, California in the early 1990s. They were photographed at the annual Memorial Day fly-past that many of the pilots from Schellville perform annually for the patients living in the Veterans Hospital in nearby Petaluma.

Formed in late 1928, the Great Lakes Aircraft Corp. took over the plant formerly occupied by the Glenn L. Martin Co. in Cleveland, Ohio. There was a swept-wing and a straight-wing version of the Great Lakes biplane, often called the 'Sport' and designed by Charles W. Meyers formerly of Waco.

Initial production was between 1929 and 1932.

The formal launch of the Great Lakes took place in March 1929 at the Detroit Air Show. The initial model had an in-line, air-cooled 85-hp Cirrus Mk 3 engine, but it was quickly replaced by a more powerful 100-hp Cirrus.

Meyers had been racing a custom version of the Great Lakes with some success and soon the company logged more than 700 orders. But the 1929 stock market crash put things back in proportion. In fact, by 1932 GLAC had built 264 aircraft. Several enterprising owners retrofit their Great Lakes with 145- and 185-hp Warner radials.

John G. 'Tex' Rankin mastered the outside loop, first in a Waco and then in 1930 in a Great Lakes; he won many other aerobatic trophies flying a Great Lakes during the Thirties. Texan Frank Price took up the banner where Rankin left off and in 1960, entirely at his own expense, shipped his 185-hp Warner-powered Great Lakes to Bratislava, Czechoslovakia to become the sole American to compete at the World Aerobatic Championships.

Doug Champlin resurrected production of the Great Lakes in 1972 at Wichita, Kansas, although prior to this, the type had been available as a reduced-scale homebuilt. Windward Aviation, Inc. of Enid, Oklahoma purchased the company and by 1978, manufactured a further 134 Great Lakes biplanes.

Bill Ewertz flying his Great Lakes Biplane (GPJ).

Above: His and Hers Great Lakes Biplane duo, Bill Ewertz and his wife Jan (GPJ).

Below: First built in 1929, Great Lakes Biplane production continued off and on until the 1980s (GPJ).

Stearman biplane in formation with the
Ewertzs' two Great Lakes Biplanes over
Petaluma (GPJ).

New Standard D-25A (1930)

NC930V is operated by Beagle Air Tours giving pleasure flights at airshows and fly-ins throughout the American South. Pictured at the National Biplane Association Fly-In at Bartlesville in 1995 and at Sun 'n Fun in Florida in 1997.

Charles H. Day designed Standard trainers during WW I. His Model D-24 in the 1920s was the first for the civil market. Built in Paterson, New Jersey, it was powered by a 180-hp Hispano-Suiza E eight-cyliner radial engine. Intended primarily for pleasure flight work, the D-24 had its pilot seated behind up to four passengers in the front open cockpit.

Developing this theme, the D-25A of 1928 was similar in design, but powered by a 220-hp air-cooled Wright Whirlwind J5 radial. The D-25A received its type certificate (No.108) in February 1929 and a total of about 65 were delivered before New Standard ceased trading in 1930.

Several D-25As were sold to Alaskan Airways for freight and passenger operations. Many served as barnstormers (the Model D-30 was fitted with floats) and as the cropdusting industry developed, several were adapted to the chore, their 1,390-pound useful payload making the New Standard D-25A one of the biggest load-lifters of its time. Most of the eight or ten built during a revival of production between 1933 and '37 flew as dusters.

The New Standard was also distinguished by a unique sesquiplane arrangement, the bulk of the lift coming from the huge 45-foot upper wing, which contributed 69% of the aircraft's 350-square feet of wing area. A new aircraft retailed for $9,750 in 1929.

Three are known to survive today, all being used for pleasure flights. One flies at Old Rhinebeck Aerodrome in Rhinebeck, New York; another is under restoration by its owner, Hugh Bikle, in Hollister, California; and the third is the Beagle Air Tours aircraft. The chance to ride in a New Standard D-25A for a modest $25 at an airshow is an opportunity that should not be missed.

Beagle Air Tours' well-known New Standard D-25A giving pleasure flights at Florida's Sun 'n Fun (GPJ).

A wave from the New Standard pilot as it departs Bartlesville, Oklahoma (GPJ).

A 45ft upper wing span gives the New Standard tremendous load lifting capability (GPJ).

Stearman 4E 'Junior Speedmail' (1930)

Owned by Reno, Nevada, Cadillac dealer Ben Scott, this Stearman 4E 'Junior Speedmail' was bought brand-new by his father, William Keith Scott, in 1930 for the then-hefty sum of $18,107.50.

When Scott Sr ordered the plane from the Stearman Aircraft Co. of Wichita, Kansas on 12 November, 1929, he asked for all the options: dual controls and instrumentation (since removed), electric starter, radio, retracting landing lights, flare tubes for night-landing flares, wheel spats, reserve fuel tank and a relief tube. Called the 'Bull Stearman' because of its 450-hp Pratt & Whitney Wasp SC-1 engine, the 4E could fly nonstop from Reno to Los Angeles.

Its fuselage emblazoned with a wolf's head inspired by the University of Nevada's mascot, NC663K took its place in the Scott Motor Co. fleet, which included another Stearman, a Fokker F10 and a Ford Trimotor. Scott Sr flew the plane for 12 years, then sold it in 1942.

After leaving Reno, NC663K became a cropduster and passed through several owners before finally being retired and left outside to rot. It was rescued by antique aircraft collector Robert Penny of Los Angeles in 1968. Penny spent the next two years restoring it with the help of Ansel Smith, the same mechanic who maintained it for Scott from 1930 to 1942.

NC663K's first post-restoration flight in 1970 was witnessed by the legendary Lloyd Stearman, the man who designed it. As he watched the elegant biplane take to the air, Stearman repeated what he'd once said about the Model 4E more than 40 years earlier, calling it 'the finest airplane we ever built'. Indeed it was: larger than most biplanes and faster than the military pursuit planes of the day.

Penny displayed NC663K at airshows on the West Coast for two years, then sold it in 1972 to Dan Wine, a United Air Lines captain in Denver, Colorado. Wine lavished the rare Stearman (of 40 Model 4 Stearmans built, only 11 were 4Es and NC663K was the only one flying at the time) with attention and restored it for the second time in its life.

In the 1980s, a friend sent Ben Scott a newspaper article about his father's old plane, which led him to contact Wine about buying it. He hadn't intended to sell the plane but when he got the proverbial offer he couldn't refuse, Wine relented. In October 1985, he delivered the Stearman to Scott in Reno. The first person to fly in it after its return was Scott Sr. Reunited with the plane he sold 55 years earlier, he took his first ride in it as a passenger at the age of 81.

Twelve years later, Ben Scott carries on the family tradition: running Reno's top Cadillac-Buick-Land Rover dealership and flying NC663K. He's logged 1,200 hours in the air to date, 400 of them in the Stearman, which can be seen at the Yesterday's Flyers Museum on Carson City Airport.

Even on the ground, the classic lines of the Stearman 4E 'Junior Speedmail' are ample proof of why designer Lloyd Stearman called it 'the finest plane we ever built' (CRS).

Owner Ben Scott cruising the same route between Los Angeles and Reno that his father flew when he owned NC663K back in 1930 (CRS).

Opposite: Business end of the 'Bull Stearman,' so named because of the powerful 450-hp Pratt & Whitney Wasp SC-1 engine up front (CRS).

A massive 'Junior Speedmail' cost $18,107 new in 1930 but is worth about ten times that in today's antique airplane market (CRS).

Stearman 4-CM-1 'Senior Speedmail' (1931)

Addison Pemberton's Stearman 4-DM 'Senior Speedmail' started life as a 300-hp Wright R-975-powered Stearman 4-CM-1, but was converted to a Model 4-DM with the addition of a 450-hp Pratt & Whitney R-985 Wasp Junior engine.

Now based in Spokane, Washington, NC485W rolled out of the Stearman Aircraft plant in Wichita, Kansas in 1931. One of a dozen 4-CM-1s ordered by American Airlines, it flew the commercial air mail route between St. Louis, Chicago, Evansville and Atlanta until 1933, when it was modified with dual controls and converted to an instrument trainer.

It left airline service in 1937 and began a second career as a cropduster in Northern California. By 1959, it had logged more than 6,000 punishing hours and was retired and put in storage. Thirty years later, a tattered basketcase, the Stearman was purchased by Addison Pemberton, an airplane aficionado who lived in San Diego, California at the time.

Pemberton's first task in restoring NC485W was getting the fuselage back from Topeka, Kansas, where it had been shipped by the plane's previous owner, well-known warbird collector, David Tallichet, whose plans to restore it never came to fruition. With the help of friends, Pemberton spent three years restoring the plane to museum-quality flying condition. Since its first post-restoration flight in May 1992, it has kept busy attending airshows and fly-ins all over the West Coast.

In September 1993, Pemberton and his two sons teamed up with the owner of another 'Senior Speedmail' to commemorate the 75th anniversary of air mail service in the United States. Flying in formation, they retraced the original transcontinental air mail route, C.A.M. 18, from Reno to Iowa City.

NC485W is one of only three 'Senior Speedmails' known to exist. It was photographed in August 1993 north of San Diego.

The pride of antique aircraft collector Addison Pemberton's fleet is this beautifully maintained 1931 Stearman 4-CM-1 (CRS).

Above: Aptly named the 'Senior Speedmail', Addison Pemberton's Stearman 4-CM-1 now carries two passengers up front where the mail used to be carried (CRS).

Below: Big brother to the Stearman 4E was the Model 4-CM-1 'Senior Speedmail' shown here in authentic American Airlines colours, circa 1933 (CRS).

Flying an air mail route over middle
America, circa 1933? No, a weekend outing
nearing Ramona, California, circa 1995
(CRS).

Waco QDC-2 (1932) and other Wacos (VIC, YMF and UKC)

NC12438 is owned by Alan Buchner of Fresno, California. In June of 1996, the beautifully restored cabin Waco won California's top antique prize, the Merced Mayors Trophy, then went on to win a top antique award at Oshkosh in August.

The QDC-2 debuted in 1931, although this particular example was rolled out the following year. Buchner found the Waco's remains in a barn in Merced, California in 1972 and whilst researching it, discovered it had been owned and flown by his father, Les Buchner, in Bakersfield between March and July 1938. Buchner started serious restoration of the aircraft in 1981 and it flew again in early 1996.

The name Waco was coined in 1919-20 when Sam Junkin and Clayton Bruker decided to build a new aircraft capable of barnstorming and carrying passengers alongside two recently rebuilt Canuck biplanes. George E. 'Buck' Weaver, a well-known Ohio pilot, teamed with Brukner and Junkin and arranged local financing for the project. They formed a company in Lorain, Ohio and decided to call it the Weaver Aircraft Company, hence Waco.

In 1922, Junkin and Bruker saw an opportunity to move to better premises in Troy, Ohio, where they established the Advance Aircraft Company. The Weaver Aircraft Company ceased to exist, but even in this short time, the name Waco for the company's aircraft stuck.

Wacos used a notoriously complex system of type designations from 1927 on, the first letter indicating the engine type, the second the wing design and the third the aircraft type. Thus, the four-seat QDC-2 has a 165-hp Continental A-70-2 radial engine (Q), a straight biplane wing configuration (D) and was the C or cabin model; the 2 denotes the second year of production, most Waco QDCs being built in 1931. NC12438 (s/n 3579) was one of the last of this marque built.

This first production cabin Waco was designed by Brukner and A. Francis Arcier and was introduced in March 1931, with a total of 32 examples built. Between 1920 and 1940, the Waco factory produced more than 3,000 aircraft, all but one (the Waco RPT) biplanes.

Fresh from a superb 15-year restoration, Alan Buchner's Waco QDC-2 (GPJ).

Opposite: Jon Aldrich's 1933 Waco UIC (NC13563) with Waco QDC-2 beyond – note the different engine cowls (GPJ).

This 1934 Waco YMF is one of 24 built. It was flown in the early 1990s by Dave Brannon on tourist pleasure flips from Kissimmee airport, near Orlando, Florida. It's finished in the colours of the Halliburton Oil Co. who used the aircraft to ferry personnel and spares to oil well sites in Texas and Oklahoma. Brand new examples of the Waco YMF can still be purchased in 1999 from the Classic Aircraft Co. of Lansing, Michigan.

Classic lines of a 1930s cabin Waco biplane (GPJ).

Based in the UK in the early 1990s, Paul McConnell's Waco UKC-S NC15214 (GPJ).

Right: Super cabin interior restoration of Alan Buchner's Waco QDC-2 – note the period instrumentation and throw-over control yoke (GPJ).

Brown B-2 Replica (1934) and other period replicas

N255Y is one of the many beautiful replicas built in Bill Turner's workshops at Flabob Airport in Rubidoux, California under the trading name of Repeat Aircraft. Turner has built a number of Golden Age air racer replicas for museums and the Hollywood film industry. This copy of Roy Minor's *Miss Los Angeles* is one of those and was completed with considerable assistance from homebuilt aircraft designer Ed Marquart.

Built in the late 1980s, it was requisitioned, along with Turner's replicas of a Miles & Atwood Special, a Wedell-Williams racer and a Gee Bee Sportster Model Z, for the 1991 Disney adventure movie *The Rocketeer*.

Also illustrated are other aircraft produced by Repeat Aircraft during the 1990s, including a re-build of the 1930 Thompson racer; NR2Y, the Howard DGA-3 *Pete*, and the most ambitious replica yet, built for Tom Wathen, the DH.88 Comet *Grosvenor House*, one of three that competed in the 1934 London-to-Melbourne Air Race.

A development of Lawrence W. Brown's Brown B-1 built in 1933, the B-2 made it first appearance at the 1934 National Air Races in Cleveland, Ohio. It debuted in the Greve Trophy Race, a contest for aircraft with engines of 550-cubic-inch displacement or less (four- or six-cylinder Menascos or Cirrus engines were fitted to the aircraft). The winner of the Greve was determined by a point system: each pilot, flying the same aeroplane in three races or heats, was credited with five points for first place, four for second, three for third, etc.

Flown by Roy Minor in this first event, the Brown B-2 came in fifth at an average speed of 213.25 mph. The winner was Lee Miles in his 225-hp Menasco-powered Miles & Atwood Special. *Miss Los Angeles* also participated in the Thompson Trophy Race in Cleveland in 1934, coming in second at a speed of 214.9 mph.

Flown by a number of pilots, the Brown B-2 participated in many air races throughout the 1930s, including the 1936 Thompson Trophy Race flown by McKeen. It ended its illustrious career in the September 1939 Greve Trophy Race when it crashed at the scattering pylon, killing pilot Lee Williams.

Bill Turner flying his Brown B-2 replica in 1990 (GPJ).

Opposite: Named *Miss Los Angeles*, the original Brown B-2 raced regularly in the US between 1934 and '39 (GPJ).

Above: Another of Bill Turner's superb restorations at his Flabob-based Repeat Aircraft Company is the Howard DGA-3 *Pete*, here flown by Robin Reid (GPJ).

Below: A superb airworthy replica of a classic British aircraft of the 1930s, but built in California by Bill Turner for Tom Wathen, the DH.88 Comet, *Grosvenor House* (GPJ).

Monocoupe 110 Replica (1934)

NC2064 is a replica of a late production Monocoupe 110 built by retired schoolteacher Fred Ludtke from original 1930's plans and powered by a 165-hp Warner Super Scarab engine. First flown in 1988 near Ludtke's home in Freeland, Washington, the plane was named *Spirit of Dynamite* and given the same registration as Pete Brooks' original 1934 aircraft.

Brooks was a well-known record-breaking aerobatic and display pilot who flew a 145-hp Warner-powered clipped-wing Monocoupe 110 in the 1930s. About 50 Model 110s were built, most with 125-hp Warner engines, but five of them with 125-hp Kinners. One was used by race pilot Jack Wright, who set a world speed record of 167.9 mph in his Monocoupe.

Ludtke restored a Monocoupe 90A in 1961 and flew it on the West Coast airshow circuit for 18 years before reluctantly selling it in 1983. When withdrawal symptoms became too much to bear, he decided to build this beautiful replica as a replacement. Unfortunately, it crashed in the Fall of 1994 and was destroyed, Ludtk's son escaping with only minor injuries.

Monocoupes were conceived by Clayton Folkerts and Donald Luscombe. When the very first Monocoupe was flown at Moline, Illinois on 1 April, 1927, it was a departure from the norm because it was a high-wing cabin monoplane. The 60-hp Veile radial engine was fitted to a production run of more than 350 examples built starting in early 1928.

Monocoupe designs continued to be built throughout the 1930s and '40s, some were even delivered to the Free French during WW II. The very last aircraft, a 115-hp Lycoming-powered Monocoupe Model 90AL-115 was built in 1950.

In 1999 Aviat Aircraft announced plans to build modernised versions of the Monocoupe 110 Special but using a 200-hp Lycoming AE10-360 instead of the 145 to 200-hp Warner radials.

With smoke on, Fred Ludtke flew many air shows with his Monocoupe 110 Replica (GPJ).

An exact replica of the 1934 original Monocoupe 110 (GPJ).

Fred Ludtke with his 1990s version of *Spirit of Dynamite* (GPJ).

Opposite: Unfortunately this aircraft crashed in Washington State in 1994 (GPJ).

Fleetwing F-4 Seabird (1936)

NC16793 was owned and flown for more than 30 years by Los Angeles-based Channing Clark at the time these photos were taken in 1994.

In early 1960, Clark heard about the wreck of a stainless-steel Fleetwing Seabird (CF-BGZ) located somewhere in British Columbia, Canada. In October 1963, after many months of travel and negotiations, the plane became his and he shipped it back home to the L.A. suburb of Glendale. Helped by Norm Neuls, Clark undertook a four-year restoration of the Seabird at Glendale College, where he taught aeronautical engineering.

This F-4 was the first of only six Seabirds built by Fleetwings, Inc. in Bristol, Pennsylvania, the other five being designated F-5s. Since its first flight in 1936, this aircraft has made several appearances on the silver screen, most recently alongside some of Bill Turner's Repeat Aircraft race replicas in the 1991 film *The Rocketeer*.

A Seabird cost $20,000 new, a very expensive luxury, even in 1936. Designed as an aerial yacht that would 'last forever', its construction was unique, being almost entirely spot-welded stainless steel, including the hull, skin, spars and wing ribs. A difficult cockpit to get into, it featured four seats and a Beech Bonanza-style throw-over control yoke.

Distinguished by the single 300-hp Jacobs 755 A-2 radial engine mounted on faired struts above the cockpit, the Seabird's cruise speed is a moderate 100 mph, with an endurance of three hours, burning 13 gallons of fuel per hour.

According to Clark, it is 'quite a handful to fly, a bit like flying two aircraft simultaneously'. Apparently, when power is cut, the Seabird reacts the opposite to most aircraft – instead of the nose dropping, it rises, making the aircraft extremely difficult to land.

Only two of the six Seabirds survive today: NC16793 shown here and the third example built, NC19191, owned by Blake Oliver and based in Daytona Beach, Florida. It is currently valued at close to $500,000.

Below: One of only two surviving Seabirds from the six built in 1936/37 (GPJ).

Opposite above: Unique stainless steel skinning of the Seabird glistens in the California sun (GPJ).

Opposite below: Channing Clark's 'office' in the Seabird, throw-over control yoke and lots of varnished wood (GPJ).

Ryan STA (1936)

NC16039 (s/n 128), sometimes called the 'Super Sport', was restored by Theodore 'Ted' Babini, who based the aircraft at Schellville Airport, north of San Francisco, California. A dedicated and fanatical antique aeroplane restorer, he also owned a 1936 Monocoupe 90A and a 1929 Fleet 2. After restoring his Ryan STA in 1990, it won the prestigious Mayors Trophy at that year's Merced Antique Aircraft Fly-In.

This aircraft was flown by the famous John 'Tex' Rankin and 'Put' Humphreys, both of whom performed regularly with Bob Wilson's Hollywood Air Aces airshow act in the 1930s. Rankin set an altitude record for light aircraft in an STA in 1935, climbing to 19,800 feet over Florida and also won the International Aerobatic Championships in this STA in 1937.

In 1939, this aircraft crashed and overturned in a field at Santa Rosa, close to where Babini lives. It wasn't seriously damaged and was soon flying again. NC16039 ceased its first flying career in 1973 and became an exhibit in the Hill County Flying Lady Air Museum in Morgan Hill, California. By 1985 it had moved to Fremont, California and deteriorated badly, with layers of dust and serious corrosion to the upper fuselage. In May 1985, Babini found the basketcase, bought it and started the five-year rebuild and restoration of this historic aircraft.

Ryan Aeronautical Co. was based at Lindbergh Field in San Diego, California on the site of San Diego's commercial airport, Lindbergh Field. The STA was developed from the similar-looking Ryan ST and became one of the first successful, widely built monoplanes in the U.S.

It was fitted with a 125-hp Menasco C-4 inverted inline engine, had tandem open cockpits, an oval-shaped monocoque structure covered in alloy sheet metal, a solid spruce main spar, metal wing ribs and a metal-covered leading edge with the remainder of the wing fabric-covered. The Ryan STA has a maximum speed of 150 mph at sea level and a normal cruise, at 75% power, of 127 mph.

About 79 Ryan STAs were built and initially sold for $3,985 or for $4,685 in a package deal that included training to an Airline Transport licence. Still considered one of the all-time classics, enthusiastic homebuilders can purchase sets of Ryan STA plans to build their very own replica STA from Ev Cassagneres of Cheshire, Connecticut.

Ted Babini, master classic aircraft restorer, in flying gear with his newly completed Ryan STA in 1990. Babini died in December 1998 at the age of 75 (GPJ).

Above: Once flown by Tex Rankin, this Ryan STA was found by Babini as a 'basketcase' in 1985 (GPJ).

Below: About 79 Ryan STAs were built at Lindbergh Field, San Diego (GPJ).

Arriving at Watsonville, California for the annual Memorial Weekend Fly-In, Ted Babini in his Ryan STA (GPJ).

Stinson Reliant SR-7B (1936)

Now one of the best looking Stinson Reliants around is this 1936 Model SR-7B, owned by retired American Airlines captain Joe Ciabattoni of Upland, California. When he bought NC15173 in 1976, it was a basketcase that took nine years to restore. However, when it was completed in July 1985, it won the coveted Grand Champion Antique award at the Watsonville Antique Fly-In, the first of many trophies it would win.

With its trademark double-tapered wing designed by Robert Hall and C.R. Irvine, NC15173 (s/n 9653) was the third SR-7B off the Stinson assembly line in Detroit back in 1936. But because the first and second aircraft were destroyed, it is now the oldest example of its kind flying.

The SR-7B was powered by a nine-cylinder, 245-hp Lycoming R-680-6 radial turning a constant-speed Lycoming-Smith propeller. The combination gave the SR-7B a top speed of 145 mph and a cruise speed of 138 – impressive figures for a single-engine airplane that could carry four people and 100 pounds of baggage.

Joe Ciabattoni shows off the classic 'gull wing' of his 1936 Stinson SR-7B Reliant over the desert near his home base in Upland, Southern California (CRS).

Aeronca LC (1937)

This extremely rare Aeronca LC belongs to 76-year-old Marc Herman of Shadow Hills, California. Powered by a five-cylinder, 90-hp Warner Scarab Jr radial, it's one of 66 Model LCs built by Aeronca, the Aeronautical Corporation of America, at Lunken Airport in Cincinnati, Ohio between 1936 and '39. And according to Herman, who spent nearly 25 years restoring it, it's the only one of seven on the FAA register still flying.

Herman first laid eyes on the airplane in 1973 when a friend rented space in his hangar at Whiteman Airport north of Los Angeles and brought the hulk of an Aeronca LC with him. Eighteen years later, it still wasn't finished, so after the owner died, Herman obtained the plane.

It took Herman and a band of helpers the next seven years to get the Aeronca airworthy. Along the way, the Warner engine was zero-timed and plenty of new metal was bent for the wing leading edges and the front half of the landing gear 'boots'.

'We put new trailing edges on the wings but just about everything else is original, including the ring cowling and the 12-ply piece of plywood that is the 1937 equivalent of a rubber Lord shock mount for the engine', explained Herman.

One of the people invited to watch the plane's first post-restoration flight was 82-year-old Jim Cullen, who owned the Aeronca back in 1939 when it was nearly brand-new. Cullen wrecked his beloved *Josephine* (the name of the heroine in a song about a flying machine) during a night take-off from the airport at Telegraph & Atlantic Avenues in Los Angeles.

'The plane cartwheeled, leaving pieces of the right wing and engine in a circle around the bent fuselage when it finally came to rest', he said. 'No one was badly hurt, so we rebuilt the plane and eventually sold it for $350', he recalled.

Owner Marc Herman shows off his just-completed Aeronca LC over the rugged hills behind his home field, Whiteman Airpark, near Los Angeles (CRS).

The extremely rare Model LC is an Aeronca like no other – low wing, radial engine, spatted wheels and side-by-side seating (CRS).

With a 90-hp, five-cylinder Warner Scarab Junior radial engine and 36-foot wingspan, the LC cruises at an even 100 mph (CRS).

Lockheed 12A (1938)

This meticulously restored 1938 Lockheed 12A Electra Junior belongs to United Airlines 767 captain Pat Donovan of Henderson, Nevada. In 1988, he made a visit to San Marcos, Texas to check out rumors of a twin-tail Lockheed sitting in a hangar at a small airfield there. A few months later, after a couple of local mechanics put the plane back in one piece, Donovan and a friend ferried it home to Arlington, Washington, trailing oil and engine parts all the way.

Once the Lockheed was safely ensconced in a hangar at Boeing Field, Donovan and his wife Ria spent the next five years tearing it down and rebuilding it. The tedious work was interrupted by occasional jaunts around the world in search of Lockheed parts. One treasure trove was discovered in a cropduster's hangar in the south Texas town of Edinburg. Although Donovan nearly collapsed when the man told

him he'd just sold the Lockheed 12 used in the movie *Casablanca* to Walt Disney World, he still picked up a number of useful items.

In early 1992, three and a half years into the restoration, Donovan obtained another cache of parts from a man who had two Lockheed 12s in St Tropez, France. The restored NC14999 (s/n 1252) made its first flight in 1994. There were some engine problems initially, but those were cured with a new pair of overhauled Pratt & Whitney R-985s from Kenmore Harbor Air in Seattle. A collapsed left main gear caused more problems, but that too has been repaired and the plane is flying once again.

Lockheed followed up its successful Lockheed 10 Electra series with the lookalike Model 12 Electra Jr. With very similar lines but slightly smaller than its predecessor, the Lockheed 12A was the world's fastest twin-engine

transport when it was introduced in November 1936. Race pilot Milo Burcham was so impressed with the plane's speed and snappy handling that he flew one in the 1937 Bendix Trophy Air Race, finishing a respectable fifth.

Because it could carry only six passengers, the 12 found only limited success with the airlines. However, it was a big hit as an executive transport, especially with oil companies, who considered a well-appointed Lockheed 12 an important status symbol. For this role, many 12s had customized club interiors installed, reducing seating to 3 or 4 passengers but increasing fuel capacity to 200 gallons and range to more than 1,000 miles.

Some 129 Lockheed 12As were built. (Only two Lockheed 12Bs – the same plane but powered by a pair of 420-hp Wright R-975-E3 engines – were built, both as utility transports for the Argentine Army.)

Too small to be a proper airliner, the Lockheed 12A quickly became the ultimate in executive air transport when it was introduced in 1938 (CRS).

Known as the 'Electra Junior' after its predecessor, the Lockheed Model 10, the 12A was powered by a pair of 400-hp Pratt & Whitney R-985 Wasp Juniors (CRS).

The instrument panel is beautiful in its simplicity, but the cockpit of the Lockheed 12A is a tight squeeze, no matter what the size of the crew (CRS).

Profile view of the Model 12A belies its relatively dainty size for an eight-passenger plane: 36.4 feet long, 9.8 feet tall and a wingspan of 49.5 feet (CRS).

Owner Pat Donovan cuts a swath across the wide-ranging wheatfields of central Washington state at a cruise speed of 210 mph (CRS).

The elegant lines of Lockheed's Model 12A made it a favourite of both oil companies and fans of art deco design (CRS).

About the only strike against the Lockheed 12A is the noise of its propellers as the tips go supersonic even at economy cruise speed (CRS).

Rose A-1 Parakeet (1938)

NC18252 was owned by Marvin Bein of Clear Lake Shores, Texas when photographed at the National Biplane Association Fly-In at Bartlesville, Oklahoma. It is now owned by Harold Stieber of Brownwood, Texas.

This Parakeet is one of 11 built in the 1930s by Jack W. Rose's Rose Aeroplane & Motor Company in Chicago, Illinois. It is fitted with a 65-hp Continental engine and can cruise at 85-95 mph. It is one of three or possibly four original 1930's Parakeets that still survive.

Nine of the original 11 Parakeets were built between 1936 and 1938. The prototype (NX-12084), underpowered with a 28-hp Heath B4 engine, was built in 1929; NX-13677, powered by a 37-hp Continental A-40, was built in 1934.

Their structure was typical American, with a steel-tube fuselage covered with fabric, wooden decking and wood-and-fabric flying surfaces. Emphasizing its small size was a wingspan of only 20 feet. The near symmetrical airfoil was also a Rose design.

The first five Parakeets were powered by 37-hp Continental engines. A 50-hp Franklin-powered example was also completed before the Continental A-65 and A-85 engines became available.

Rose invested around $250,000 in designing, developing and building his Parakeets and sold them, ready-to-fly, for a mere $1,475.

An incomplete Rose-built Parakeet was stored until after WW II and finished as an 'Experimental' aircraft. An instant hit, it was later offered as a plans-built design for homebuilders. In 1963, Doug Rhinehart of Farmington, New Mexico acquired three original Parakeets plus the type certificate, intending to recertificate the type for limited production. This never materialised as he died in 1978, but at least five Parakeets still survive.

Marvin Bein flying his tiny Parakeet biplane in Oklahoma in 1995 (GPJ).

Opposite above: With a 20ft wingspan and 65hp Continental engine, the Parakeet is very compact (GPJ).

Opposite below: The Parakeet has a steel tube fuselage covered with fabric (GPJ).

Waco EGC-8 (1939)

Les Whittlesey bases his beautiful cabin Waco at the famed Chino Airport in Southern California. Although it's an EGC-8, it rolled off the Waco Aircraft Co. production line in Troy, Ohio as an AGC-8 Custom Cabin. NC53E (s/n 5069) was one of eight Jacobs-powered AGC-8s delivered to the new Civil Aeronautics Authority in 1939.

Waco built its AGC-8s to order and hand-crafted them to each customer's specific requirements. But sometime during the seven years it was operated by CAA regional inspectors, NC53E was upgraded to a Model EGC-8 by replacing the 300-hp Jacobs L-6 with a more-powerful seven-cylinder, 320-hp Wright R760E-2.

When NC53E left the CAA in 1946, it passed through several owners, including movie star Jackie Cooper, before Les' father bought it in 1973. Whittlesey Sr flew it for 10 years then sold it to Les, who hung a new engine on it and continued flying it until November 1988. By then, the plane was beginning to show its age, prompting Les to ground it for a total restoration.

Like most such undertakings, it took longer than expected, but four and a half years later, NC53E rolled out of Whittlesey's hangar in better-than-new condition. Whittlesey flies the Waco often and it turns heads everywhere it goes.

'It's a mixed blessing', he says, 'because with everyone watching, there's a lot of pressure to make good landings and the Waco is a little tricky to land. It's a really fun airplane to fly. It handles like a J-3 Cub at slow airspeeds but is quite fast for a biplane'.

The Waco Aircraft Company was one of the most prolific American aircraft manufacturers of the 1930s and '40s and almost all of its planes were as handsome as this Model ECG-8 (CRS).

This 1939 Waco ECG-8 was first operated by the Civil Aeronautics Authority, the predecessor to today's Federal Aviation Administration (CRS).

Opposite: Cabin window rolled down, owner Les Whittlesey cruises the central California wine country accompanied by the roar of his Waco's 320-hp Wright R760 radial (CRS).

The Waco's Hamilton-Standard propeller is just a blurred, silvery disk as owner Les Whittlesey warms up the Wright radial prior to takeoff (CRS).

Typical of cabin Wacos, the ECG-8 handles like a J-3 Cub at slow speeds, yet easily outruns many modern Cessnas with its 140-mph cruise speed (CRS).

Banking away from the camera ship, Les Whittlesey proves that cabin Wacos look good from any angle (CRS).

Aeronca 65-TL (1940)

NC314432 was built in 1940 and signed off from the factory at Lunken Airport in Cincinnati, Ohio on 15 September, 1940. Originally intended for delivery to the Defense Plant Corp., it was requisitioned for the Civilian Pilot Training Program and assigned to a flight school in Pendleton, Oregon.

It was flown by the University of Washington before passing to the Flying Guardsmen Aero Club of Washington in 1953. Stored between then and 1985, it was deteriorating rapidly when discovered and rescued by Ron Englund, an Oregon-based aircraft mechanic and flight instructor.

The restoration was finally completed in April 1993. When Englund found the basketcase Aeronca, it had only 1,000 hours total time; in the three years since he restored it, he put about 100 hours a year on it. The aircraft was photographed in June 1997 at Merced, California. In 1998 Englund flew this aircraft to Oshkosh.

The better-known side-by-side two-seat Aeronca Chief was a development of the 1938 Aeronca 50-L and was fitted with a 65-hp Lycoming engine. Certificated in October 1938, many were delivered to the U.S. Army Air Corps.

James A. Weagle, Aeronca's chief designer, thought a light, tandem-seat version was what a lot of flying schools and the CPTP wanted. In March 1940, Aeronca announced three versions of their new Aeronca: the 65-TC (Continental A-65-7), the 65-TF (Franklin 4AC-176-B2) and the 65-TL (Lycoming O-145-B1). A total of 232 65-TLs were built, with a further 238 of the TC and TFs. Other variants followed: the 65-TAC, 65-TAF and 65-TAL adding another 340 examples. A total of nearly 900 civil aircraft of the type were built, as well as 1,414 military deliveries of the Aeronca L-3 version.

A new Aeronca 65-TL sold for $1,650 in 1940, a price reduced to $1,425 because of the many competitors around at the time. Ron Englund's restoration is one of the finest examples of about 100 of the type still extant.

Ron Englund's superb Aeronca 65-TL Tandem (GPJ).

Tandem 2-seater, the Aeronca 65-TL with restorer Ron Englund at the controls (GPJ).

Below: Many different engines were fitted to Aeronca 65s – this is a Lycoming O-145-B1 (GPJ).

Slow but steady progress at 75–80mph, the cruise speed of the Aeronca 65-TL (GPJ).

A single-right/starboard door provides access to the two tandem seats (GPJ).

Cessna C-165 Airmaster (1940)

NC237E is owned by Ken Coe of Livermore, California, a retired Western and Delta Air Lines Boeing 737 captain.

When this Airmaster was new in 1940, it was bought by the Civil Aeronautics Authority, the predecessor to the current Federal Aviation Administration. Coe acquired the aircraft in 1971 and has owned it ever since. In 1994, he carried out a major restoration, including painting it in the original CAA colours as depicted in these photos taken at Merced, California in June 1996.

Cessna broke new ground in 1933 when they built the high-wing, strutless Cessna C-3 for Walt Anderson before he sold it to publisher Marcellus Murdock.

Late in 1934, Dwane Wallace, a nephew of Clyde Cessna, developed the four-seat cabin Cessna C-34 from the C-3. Powered by a 145-hp Warner Super Scarab engine, it was widely accepted as the most efficient aircraft in its class at the time. It had a 34-foot, 2-inch wingspan, a top speed of 162-mph and a cruise of 143 mph.

In 1937, Cessna introduced the slightly modified C-37, followed in 1938 by the C-38, which had a wider landing gear with bowed profile. Then came the Cessna C-145 Airmaster late in 1938 and the 165-hp Warner-powered C-165 Airmaster in 1939. Between 1939 and 1942, a total of 83 Cessna C-145s and 165s were built.

Below: Only 83 Cessna C-145 and C-165s were built (GPJ).

Above: Cessna's 1940 logo depicted on Ken Coe's Airmaster (GPJ).

Opposite: High over the Californian central valley, Ken Coe's Cessna C-165 Airmaster (GPJ).

Piper J-3C Cub (1940)

Considering he learned to fly in a Cub his CFI bought brand new in 1946, it was no surprise when 23-year-old Darren Clarkson bought this 1940 clipped-wing Piper J-3C Cub in 1996 to give instruction in.

N30244 is one of 19,888 J-3 Cubs of various models manufactured by Piper Aircraft Corp. from 1937 to 1947. More specifically, it's one of 1,881 built in 1940: a J-3C-65 powered by a 65-hp Continental A-65-1 engine. At least that's what it started out as.

Like many Cubs, N30244 has had a varied career, undergoing a number of major modifications in its 58 years. The first was a popular postwar upgrade to the Continental C-85 engine, which produced 85 hp at 2,575 rpm. Next, with the rear cabin windows and back seat replaced by a chemical hopper, it was converted into a cropduster and operated in the Restricted category.

In 1990, it was the subject of another popular mod, this one designed to turn the normally docile Cub into a sprightly aerobatic mount by radically increasing

its roll rate. As part of the Reed clipped-wing conversion, six feet was lopped off the inside of both wings, decreasing the wingspan from 35 feet to 23. Shortly after that, the plane was acquired by aerobatic legend Patty Wagstaff, who kept it until 1995.

After being damaged in a hangar collapse, it was repaired and sold to Kevin McKown of Albuquerque, N.M. Clarkson bought the plane from him in February 1997 and, except for repairs to some minor dings incurred in an off-field landing, has had nothing but fun with it.

'It's great for mild aerobatics, such as loops, rolls and spins, and for off-field STOL work', he said. 'It stalls at 35 mph with one person aboard, 45 with two. Except for the faster roll rate with the clipped wings, there's not much different between this and a standard J-3C'.

By 1939, the Cub series was an established success, with J-3s powered by 50-hp Continental, Lycoming and Franklin engines the latest in the constantly evolving line. The biggest

seller, though, was the Continental A-50-powered J-3C-50. Although Continental introduced a 65-hp version of its reliable A-50 in 1939 and called it the A-65, it wasn't until Piper's chief competitors, Aeronca and Taylorcraft, began using them that it jumped on the bandwagon.

A slight re-design and strengthening of the basic Cub design to accommodate the bigger engine resulted in the J-3C-65. Franklin and Lycoming-powered versions followed but it was the Continental-powered Cub that was to become the most popular, with examples rolling off the production line in Lock Haven, Pennsylvania in 1941 at a rate of eight airplanes a day.

Although production of J-3C-65s for the civil market was halted by America's entry into the war in 1942, production resumed in late-1945 for three more years, with another 8,252 aircraft being built. But by then, the much-anticipated post-war boom in personal aircraft sales had gone bust and the J-3C Cub was superseded by the 65- and later 90-hp PA-11 Cub Special.

Perhaps the quintessential American light plane: the legendary Piper J-3 Cub, this one a J-3C-65 with clipped wings (CRS).

Owner 23-year-old Darren Clarkson, an aeronautical technology student at Arizona State University, flies his 85-hp Cub 'just for fun' (CRS).

A shape recognised the world over – some 19,888 of William Piper's J-3 Cubs were built from 1937 to 1947 (CRS).

Owner Darren Clarkson flies his Cub past the famous Red Rock Mountains near his home base: Falcon Field in Mesa, Arizona (CRS).

Porterfield CP-65 Collegiate (1940)

This 1940 Porterfield CP-65 Collegiate owned by 63-year-old Larry Trager is one of the best-looking, most-active examples in Southern California. It's kept at Tehachapi Airport, which has a 4,035-foot runway and sits 3,996 feet up in the Tehachapi Mountains, 100 miles north of Los Angeles.

The *Skinny Bird*, as Trager calls the narrow-waisted Collegiate, rolled off the Porterfield production line in Kansas City in 1940. Of the 400 or so built, only 68 remain on the FAA register today.

NC32409's career was fairly mundane until 1959, when it crashed in El Paso, Texas. Afterwards, the damaged hulk was stored until it was rebuilt by Jim and Bob Daugherty of Clovis, New Mexico in November 1988. When Trager bought it in June 1992, even the Continental A-65-8 engine was in mint condition.

In the seven years he's owned the plane, Trager has put more than 1,000 hours on it, bringing the total airframe time up to 2,500 hours, incredibly low for a 59-year-old airplane. No hangar queen, most of that 1,000 hours has been to and from fly-ins and airshows all over the Western U.S. Considering that every flight out of Tehachapi involves challenging mountain flying, the Porterfield has acquitted itself well over the years.

Pioneer airplane-builder E.E. Porterfield Jr founded American Eagle Aircraft Corp. in Kansas City, Mo. in the mid-1920s. American Eagle absorbed Chicago-based Wallace Aircraft in 1929, and the following year, merged with Lincoln Aircraft Company of Lincoln, Neb. As a condition of the merger, Porterfield had to step down to the position of sales manager. It didn't take him long to chafe at that situation and in August 1931, he left to start his own company.

The first airplane to carry the Porterfield name was the Model 35-70 Flyabout, introduced in 1935. Although an original design, its American Eagle ancestry was obvious enough to the airplane-buying public to make it an instant success. Next off the line in 1936 came the Porterfield 35-V and 35-W, a pair of lookalike, radial-engine, tandem two-seaters.

Porterfield introduced the first Collegiate, the Continental A-50-powered Model CP-50, in 1939. Although it enjoyed moderate success, it never sold as well as the Aeroncas, Taylors and Pipers, a source of frustration to the company's head of sales: air-racing legend Col. Roscoe Turner.

The CP-50 begat the Model CP-55, powered by a 55-hp Continental A-50-8 and designed as a trainer for the Civilian Pilot Training Program. When everyone else came out with 65-hp aircraft, the CP-55 was upgraded to 65 hp.

By mid-1940, three versions of the resulting 65-hp Collegiate were in production: the Continental-powered CP-65, Lycoming-powered LP-65 and Franklin-powered FP-65. The Collegiate was also offered as a deluxe sportplane for private owners but because of the government drive to train pilots for the looming war in Europe, most of them went to flight schools as CPTP trainers.

All of the 65-hp Collegiates had a reputation for easy handling, good performance, reliability and affordable operation. CPTP instructors loved the fact that it could recover hands-off from a six-turn spin in less than one revolution.

However, in early 1942, shortly after America entered the war, the government dealt Porterfield a death

Not to be confused with its lookalike contemporaries, this is a 1940 Porterfield CP-65 Collegiate owned by Larry Trager of Tehachapi, California (CRS).

blow. After building only 400 aircraft, it was forced to halt production of the Collegiate so it could build Waco CG-4A troop gliders.

Even after 59 years of non-stop flying, owner Larry Trager says about the only maintenance he does on his Porterfield is put oil and gas in it (CRS).

Owner Larry Trager heading west over the Southern California high desert, cruising at a comfortable 95 mph (CRS).

With his Porterfield's 65-hp Continental A-65-8 screaming at 2,300 rpm, Larry Trager pulls it in tight for a close-up portrait (CRS).

Waco UPF-7 (1940)

N29946 is known affectionately as *Willie Waco* by its owner, flying dentist Aarden Valasek. Photographed in May 1990 at Schellville, California, it is finished mainly in the colours of an Army Air Corps aircraft from the Civilian Pilot Training Program, but it also bears the spoof name derived from Valasek's christian name: *Aardvark Air*.

Waco responded to the need for training pilots for the U.S. military by offering its UPF-7, an open-cockpit, tandem two-seat biplane powered by a 220-hp Wright W-670-6A engine. The Waco F-7 was used for test purposes and to secure the prestigious CPTP contract. UPF-7 production commenced in March 1940, three of the first aircraft being exported to Venezuela. CPTP aircraft were first built in July, and by September, Waco had cranked out 100 UPF-7s, their production geared to completion of three aircraft per day.

Almost as suddenly as production of the UPF-7 started, it ceased. The government asked Waco to cease production of propeller-driven aircraft in favour of urgently needed troop-carrying gliders to be towed behind Douglas C-47s. Thus was born the CG-4A troop glider.

The last UPF-7 was completed on 7 November, 1942 after production of more than 600 aircraft.

Many American pilots trained in Waco UPF-7s during the 1940s (GPJ).

The 220-hp Wright W-670-6A engine of the Waco UPF-7 (GPJ).

Aardvark over America, courtesy of flying dentist Aarden Valasek (GPJ).

With California's coastal mountains beyond, the Waco UPF-7 is safely hangared at Schellville as a Stearman biplane taxies past (GPJ).

General Aircraft G1-80 Skyfarer (1941)

Chris Cagle of Hemet, California flies a plane that is often mistaken for a botched attempt to fuse a Tri-Pacer with an Ercoupe. Neither Piper nor Ercoupe, Cagle's mount is a General Aircraft Corp. Model G1-80 Skyfarer, one of 17 built and only two survivors.

Cagle bought the twin-tailed two-seater in 1960 after he found it rotting behind a hangar at Reid-Hillview Airport in Northern California. He rescued it, restored it, then restored it again a few years ago and now flies it only occasionally.

The Skyfarer was designed by Otto C. Koppen, an aeronautics professor at the Massachusetts Institute of Technology. Originally called the Puritan, the prototype was tested in MIT's wind tunnel before its public debut in November 1939. Though it incorporated several revolutionary design principles, the Puritan did not attract much attention.

Acquired by General Aircraft Corp. of South Lowell, Massachusetts, the design was reworked and a more powerful engine installed for its introduction as the Skyfarer in 1941. The patented new design principle that distinguished Koppen's aircraft was the use of only two rather than three controls to guide the plane in flight. With two fixed vertical fins replacing the moveable rudder, lateral and directional coordination was accomplished with ailerons only. Like the Ercoupe, which arrived on the scene in April 1940, the Skyfarer was placarded as 'characteristically incapable of spinning'.

Marketing of the Skyfarer was typical pie-in-the-sky advertising: 'Imagine your car flashing over traffic jams, soaring cross-country without regard for detours, road conditions or other cares and annoyances that plague earthbound travelers! Such a thrill is yours in the new Skyfarer, the automobile of the air'.

According to the salesmen, the Skyfarer could be mastered in a few hours: 'To steer, merely turn the wheel right or left; to take off or land, set the flap lever'.

'Oh, that it was so simple, especially for someone with time in a conventional stick-and-rudder plane', says Cagle. While it can't be spun or stalled, flying a plane with no rudder does take some getting used to.

Except for the pioneering use of tricycle gear, both the Skyfarer and the Ercoupe had only a minor influence on the development of General Aviation lightplanes. Although an initial production run of 65 airplanes was planned, only 17 were completed between April-August 1941. Cagle's NC29030 (s/n 17) was the last one built, completed 15 August, 1941.

Soon after the outbreak of WW II, the Skyfarer was shelved while General Aircraft built Waco CG-4A troop gliders. In July 1943, it sold the design to Grand Rapids Industries, a consortium of Michigan-based furniture manufacturers that hoped to build a postwar version of the Skyfarer.

The effort never got off the ground and the hapless Skyfarer was sold to Tennessee Aircraft of Nashville, Tenn., then to a group of investors in LeMars, Iowa, who tried, unsuccessfully, to sell it as the Mars Skycoupe.

The Skyfarer is powered by a four-cylinder, 75-hp Lycoming GO-145-C2 geared engine turning a 77-inch-diameter Gardner wooden propeller. Cagle says the Skyfarer handles well but is no speed demon; cruise speed is about 85 mph.

Chris Cagle's 1941 General Aircraft G1-80 Skyfarer is the last flying example of a little-known breed (CRS).

The Skyfarer was one of the first light planes to feature a nosewheel instead of the more common, and much preferred, 'conventional' tailwheel (CRS).

Look closely at the Skyfarer's twin tail – like the better-known Ercoupe, there is no rudder or moveable control surface (CRS).

Powered by a 75-hp Lycoming GO-145-C2 engine, Chris Cagle's Skyfarer has a cruise speed of 92 mph (CRS).

The General Aircraft Skyfarer is a tiny two-seater, 22 feet long, 8.7 feet high and with a 31.5 foot wingspan (CRS).

Interstate S-1A Cadet (1942)

Although the Interstate Cadet isn't as well known as its contemporaries, the Aeronca Chief, Piper Cub, Porterfield Collegiate and Taylorcraft BC12, it survives in relatively large numbers today. Of the more than 300 S-1A Cadets manufactured by the Interstate Aircraft & Engineering Corp. of El Segundo, California between 1940 and 1942, about 100 of them are still flying.

NC37411, a 1942 model in authentic factory colours, belongs to Jason Williams, a 25-year-old cable-splicer for U.S. West Telephone in Mesa, Arizona. He bought the plane in 1997 to build time for a commercial and ATP licence. Of the 250 hours in his logbook, 100 are in the Cadet.

'There's no electrical system, so it has to be hand-propped but other than that, it's a joy to fly', said Williams of the slab-sided two-seater.

Were it not for the threat of war and the rush to train pilots for the military, the Cadet might not have been born. Interstate Engineering Corp. didn't start out as an airplane company, it was a subcontractor that built mechanical and hydraulic components for other people's airplanes. But when it bought a new plant that turned out to be bigger than needed, Interstate President Donald Smith took that as his cue to jump into the burgeoning aircraft manufacturing industry. After all, building airplanes for the government's Civilian Pilot Training Program was a nearly foolproof way to break into the business.

Interstate hired aeronautical engineer Ted Woolsey to design its first airplane. In a move that was typical of small companies of the day, Woolsey laid out the basic design, then turned the detail work over to students at the Wiggins Trade School. The result was the 50-hp S-1 Cadet, which made its first flight in April 1940 with test pilot 'Slim' Kidwell at the controls. Kidwell gave the plane a thumbs-up but recommended a more-powerful engine.

Thus was born the 65-hp S-1A Cadet. When it was issued a type certificate in February 1941, it became the first light plane to be manufactured on the West Coast. Cadets began rolling off the production line at a rate of one a day by May 1941, even faster a few months later. When production was halted in 1942 so that Interstate could concentrate on L-6/S-1Bs for the military, some 300 S-1As had been built, including some with 65-, 85- and 90-hp Franklin engines.

When NC37411 came off the line in 1942, it went straight to work as a primary trainer in the CPTP. Williams isn't clear on the specifics, but he thinks the plane was wrecked and repaired several times before finding its way to Missouri. Its owner flew it for a while, then in 1958, placed it in storage in a warehouse, where it remained for the next 25 years. Finally, in 1983, it was rescued and restored, remaining in Missouri until CFI Leslie Perry brought it to Arizona.

'It was worked hard early in its career', Williams allowed, 'but since 1958, it's had only about 500 hours put on it – that's only about 12-15 hours a year on average'.

At 24 feet long and with a 35.5-foot wingspan, the Interstate Cadet was much bigger than its Aeronca, Piper and Porterfield contemporaries (CRS).

Top left: Original Cadet logo on the tail of Jason Williams' S-1A, manufactured by the Interstate Aircraft & Engineering Corp. of El Segundo, California (CRS).

Top: Although a third of the 300 S-1A Cadets built from 1940 to 1942 are still flying in the US, few look as authentic as this one (CRS).

Left: With the Cadet's Continental A-65-8 engine running flat out, pals Darren Clarkson and Jason Williams slip in close for this aerial portrait (CRS).

What antique aircraft doesn't look more at home on grass than concrete? (CRS).

Beech 'Staggerwing' D17S (1944)

This Beech 'Staggerwing' is owned by Granger Haugh and is based at Fallbrook Airport, a tiny hilltop airfield 60 miles north of San Diego on the California coastline. The break behind the cowl identifies it as an early D17S rather than one of the later, extended-cowl G models.

Manufactured by Beechcraft as a D17S, s/n 6708 was delivered in 1944 to the Army Air Force, where it was designated a GB-2 and wore the military

California, who flew it for eight years.

The plane was sold again in 1971 to a couple of airline pilots from Kodiak, Alaska. After only two years, it moved south again, finally leaving the West Coast when it was purchased by Robert Dalzell of Kentucky in 1973. Dalzell spent the next 10 years restoring the plane, including zero-timing the 400-hp Pratt & Whitney R-985 Wasp Jr radial and the Hamilton Standard constant-speed prop. He also changed the

Switzerland, Peier opted to fly it there via the North Atlantic route. The trip took 26 flying hours over several days and was anything but uneventful.

He nearly lost the plane twice when ice built up on the fuel vents and starved the engine. As he glided lower and lower towards the water, the outside temperature increased enough to melt the ice and enable him to restart the engine. Once it reached Zürich, NC582 was one of only two

registration FT-478. Although the Army used it for utility and transport duties, the logbooks indicate it had only 97.6 hours on it when released from military service in 1947. The low-time beauty was quickly grabbed up by its first civilian owner: Harry Golding of Long Beach, California, who registered the plane as N1183V. In 1953, Golding sold the plane to Robert Gimblin of Colusa,

registration back to its original 1944 N number: NC582.

At the time of the rebuild, the plane had only 425 hours on the airframe. After two years of enjoying the fruits of his labour, Dalzell sold the plane to Heinz Peier, a DC-10 captain for Swissair who lived in Zürich, Switzerland. Rather than disassemble and ship the 'Staggerwing' to

A profile no aerophile can resist: bulbous spinner, big round engine, reverse-staggered wings, rounded tail – the Beechcraft 'Staggerwing' (CRS).

‘Staggerwings’ in Europe. (The other was a UC-43-BH Traveler, the military version, based at North Weald in England with Rob Lamplough.)

In 1991, Peier took a two-year sabbatical from Swissair and moved to Chino, California to restore a Grumman Goose. Because he still wanted to fly while living in the U.S., he brought the 'Staggerwing' with him – by boat this time. He sold the plane to Haugh in 1994 shortly after completing his Goose.

These aerial photos of the 'Staggerwing' were taken over the San Bernardino Mountains east of Los Angeles in March 1993 when Peier still owned it.

A 'Staggerwing' affects the senses like no other airplane. The rich leather interior and solid sound of the left-hand cabin door slamming shut immediately puts one in mind of a Cadillac El Dorado. Despite its short main gear, the cabin sits at a jaunty angle that gives an impression of speed even when it's sitting still.

As the R-985 Wasp Jr roars to life, blue-grey clouds of smoke curl up from the twin exhaust stacks beneath the cowl and hang next to the cabin for a moment before being swept away by the propwash. The smell is sweet and intoxicating and lingers for the remainder of the flight. The throaty rumble of the 400 horses warming up for the main event is music to the ear.

A ride in a 'Staggerwing' is a pleasure every pilot should experience at least once in lifetime.

From the day it rolled off the Beech production line in Wichita, Kansas and still today, the 'Staggerwing' has been considered the ultimate biplane (CRS).

No, previous owner Heinz Peier is not flying his D17S over his native Swiss Alps; it's actually the San Bernardino Mountains of Southern California (CRS).

Distinctive rounded tail and retractable tail-wheel of the Beech 'Staggerwing' (CRS).

The two basic models of the 'Staggerwing' are easily distinguished by the shape of the cowling: the early D17S like this had a break, the later G-model did not (CRS).

Douglas DC-3 (1945)

There aren't many 50-year-old former troop transports around that look as good as Classic Express Airways' DC-3. Based at John Wayne Airport in Santa Ana, the ex-RAF Dakota is owned by retired lawyer Tom Brown of Huntington Beach, Calif. He bought it in 1994 and spent two years and a small fortune restoring it to like-new condition.

Brown originally planned to use the 31-seat DC-3 to fly passengers from Los Angeles to gambling destinations like Las Vegas, Reno and Laughlin, Nevada. He has since decided that flying scheduled passenger service would be asking too much of an airplane more than a half-century old, so he's opted for less demanding, more profitable movie work and nostalgia flights to Catalina Island.

N103NA (s/n 33569) rolled off the Douglas assembly line at Santa Monica on 28 June, 1945 as a C-47B. Shortly thereafter, it went into service with the Royal Air Force in England, serving for a time as Prime Minister Winston Churchill's personal transport. Princess Elizabeth, now Queen Elizabeth, even flew on the plane three times during the war years.

After the war, the plane was shipped to Canada, where it served with the RCAF before passing through a number of private operators. Its last operators were Ilford-Riverton Airways and Air Manitoba, from whom Brown bought the plane via an aircraft dealer in Ohio.

Decked out as an executive-style luxury transport, N103NA once carried Winston Churchill and Princess Elizabeth during its service in the RAF (CRS).

Once common in American skies, the DC-3 revolutionised air transportation by making it efficient and affordable (CRS).

The logo of Classic Express Airways, which operated in Southern California, giving nostalgic sightseeing tours of the Pacific coastline and Catalina Island (CRS).

Tom Brown's DC-3 cruising north along the Pacific coastline near San Clemente, California, in 1997 (CRS).

Accompanied by the roar of its two 1,830-hp Pratt & Whitney 1830 radials, Classic Express Airways' DC-3 is in its element (CRS).

Ercoupe 415E (1946)

N3047H (s/n 3672) is owned and flown by Jack Compere, a 77-year-old disabled pilot from Paso Robles, California. He restored the plane between 1985 and 1987 and it was still in pristine condition when photographed at Merced, California in June 1997.

The Ercoupe's unique interlinked rudder and aileron controls, which eliminated the need for rudder pedals, has allowed many disabled pilots to continue flying. With a maximum gross weight of 1,450 pounds, it is powered by a 100-hp Continental O-200 engine, which gives it a maximum speed of 130 mph and a normal cruise of 110 mph.

The two-seat, twin-tail Ercoupe, its name taken from the acronym for 'Engineering and Research Corporation', was developed mainly by Fred Weick, who had been assistant chief of the NACA Aerodynamics Division. Among its revolutionary features: an inability to spin, tricycle landing gear for ease of landing in crosswinds, a fully cowled engine and a control system in which the rudders are directly linked to the ailerons for ease of control. The prototype first flew in October 1937 with Weick at the controls; before WW II intervened, 112 examples were built.

Between 1945 and 1969, a further 5,500 Ercoupes were built by a variety of companies, Jack Compere's being one of the first post-war examples. Other variants included the Forney F-1 (1958-59), the Alon A-2 (1965-67), the Mooney A-2A (1968) and the Mooney M-10 Cadet with a Mooney-style tail (1969-70). All these 1960's and '70's versions have a maximum gross weight of 1,450 pounds.

Developed by the Engineering and Research Corporation – hence the name ERCOUPE (GPJ).

Disabled Jack Compere with his 1946 Ercoupe 415E (GPJ).

Unique inter-linked rudder and ailerons controls distinguish the Ercoupe (GPJ).

Twin tails and tricycle undercarriage were unusual for the first Ercoupe in 1937 (GPJ).

Over 5,500 varied examples of the Ercoupe were built by several manufacturers between 1945 and 1970 (GPJ).

Beechcraft Model 35 Bonanza (1947 and 1948)

This beautifully maintained, completely stock 1947 Model 35 Bonanza had been owned by 83-year-old Jerry Coigny since 1969 and these photos were taken near Porterville, California in August 1995. Although he died in 1998, Coigny had been involved in aviation since 1934 when he worked for Douglas, bucking rivets on the DC-2. When he met his wife Lucy in 1938, she was the personal secretary of designer Donald Luscombe.

When Coigny bought NC3869N (s/n 1110) in 1969 for $6,000, it had only 800 hours on it. Today, with 2,000 hours on it, it's easily worth 10 times that. Manufactured in November 1947, everything about the plane is stock, except for the yoke-mounted GPS.

Because NC3869N is such a perfect example of a stock Bonanza, the Coignys were frequent guests of Olive Ann Beech at aircraft rollouts in Wichita, Kans. Another benefit to owning such a popular classic is that Beech dealers everywhere they went gave them the red-carpet treatment.

One of the plane's biggest attention-getters is its laminated wooden propeller. The electrically controlled, 88-inch-diameter, Beech-designed Roby prop may look out of place on the sleek Bonanza, but it is completely original.

During its 51-year production run, some 37 different models of Bonanzas and straight-tail Debonairs – to date, more than 17,250 aircraft – rolled off the Beech (now Raytheon Aircraft) production line in Wichita, Kansas.

The specifications for a 180-mph four-seater were drawn up by Walter Beech during WW II. The prototype Bonanza (NX80040) first flew at Wichita, Kansas in December 1945 with veteran test pilot Vern Carstens at the controls. The Model 35 was certificated in March 1947 and production began in 1947 with 1,196 examples built. Another 303 were built in 1948, bringing the total number of straight 35s produced to 1,499. The first 973 sold for $7,975, the remainder for $8,945.

Hallmarks of the 1947 Beech Model 35 Bonanza were the laminated wood prop, the signature V-tail and the retractable tricycle gear (CRS).

Basically unchanged in 50 years, owner Jerry Coigny's aeroplane is a rare example of a totally stock Model 35 Bonanza (CRS).

Owner Jerry Coigny flew his Bonanza from his Timberline Ranch Air Strip, a 2,400-foot grass strip 4,000 feet up in the Sierra Nevada Mountains (CRS).

The late Jerry Coigny was still flying his Bonanza, in impeccable formation for this photo shoot, at the age of 85 (CRS).

Over flat Dutch countryside this 1948 Beechcraft 35 Bonanza was 'signed off' at the factory by Walter Beech himself (GPJ).

German registered non-stock Bonanza with Enrico Evers at the controls. It sold for $9,445 when new in 1948 (GPJ).

With additional rear cabin windows this Bonanza has been totally refurbished by German Beechcraft agents HLW of Bremen (GPJ).

Enrico Evers steps aboard his Bonanza at Lelystad, Holland. This aircraft has a 225-hp Continental 0-300-8 (GPJ).

Grumman G-73 Mallard (1947)

This Mallard amphibian first appeared on the FAA register in April 1947 as N2958. By the time it was photographed in Florida at the EAA Sun 'n Fun Fly-In at Lakeland in April 1998, it was owned by Jack Bart and registered as N98BS. Its first owner was Burrus Mills, Inc. of Dallas, Texas, which used it as a corporate transport and named it *Milling Around*. It was also used occasionally during this time by Ben Bransom Charter Service.

In March 1956, it was sold to the McLouth Steel Corp. of Detroit and re-registered as N10M. By June 1975, it had accumulated 8,900 hours in the air.

Bart, who runs the Universal Attractions Agency in New York, acquired the aircraft in 1991 and christened it *Ti-Loup du Lac*. He bases it at Fort Lauderdale Executive Airport during the winter, but flies it north to Bridgeport, Connecticut during the summer.

Grumman's first post-war flying boat design, a total of 61 10-passenger Grumman G-73 Mallards were built between 1946 and 1951. This example is powered by two 600-hp Pratt & Whitney R-1340 Wasp air-cooled radials, which give it a cruise speed 180 mph at 8,000 feet and 55% power.

Most Mallards were sold as corporate transports or for bush operations, subsequently being modified for feeder-liner operations. The best known commercial operator was Florida-based Chalk's Airlines, which flew them on scheduled service between downtown Miami (Watson Island) and various islands in the Bahamas archipelago. The Chalk's Mallards were converted to PT6A turbine power in the 1980s. In fact, of the 25 or so Mallards still extant, 15 are turbine powered and 10, including Bart's, are still powered by the original Wasps.

In superb condition, Jack Bart's G-73 Mallard, over the Florida countryside (GPJ).

Still with original P&W radial engines, this G-73 Mallard is one of only about ten examples remaining with original engines (GPJ).

At 55 per cent power the Mallard's two P&W R-1340 engines give it a 180mph cruise and 1,290ft/min rate of climb (GPJ).

More ungainly on the ground than on the water or in the air, the Mallard is still a superb 'go anywhere' aircraft, seen here at the Leeward Air Ranch, near Ocala, Florida (GPJ).

Piper PA-12 Super Cruiser (1947)

N78547 is owned by retired military and corporate jet pilot Tom Watson of Corona, California. His is one of the last Super Cruisers built and is fitted with the slightly more powerful 108-hp Lycoming O-235-C1 engine.

The prototype PA-12 (NX41333), powered by a 100hp Lycoming O-235-C engine, first flew in December 1945 with Piper's C.R. Smith at the controls.

First shown at the National Aircraft Show at Cleveland, Ohio in November 1946 and promoted with the name *Taxi-Cub*, the Super Cruiser was a three-seater with a 90-mph economical cruise. Developed from the pre-war J-5C Cub Cruiser, production of which had ended in 1942, it was a step between the basic J-3 Cub and the later PA-18 Super Cub.

At the height of Super Cruiser production in March 1947, 3,000 Piper employees were completing 30 100-hp PA-12s a day and a total of nearly 700 a month. But in May 1948, production ceased almost as quickly as it had begun, with a total of just under 3,800 examples built. The hoped-for boom in post-war private flying never really materialized.

Beautifully restored Piper PA-12 Super Cruiser is regularly flown the 4,000+ miles from its California base to Oshkosh and back (GPJ).

Above: The Super Cruiser was also known as the *Taxi-Cub* when it was introduced in 1946 (GPJ).

Below: Tom Watson flying his Piper PA-12 Super Cruiser close to the foothills of the Sierra Nevada in California (GPJ).

Stinson 108 Voyager (1948)

NC97651 is owned by Dave and Debbie Cheney, who base their aircraft at Flabob Airport in Rubidoux, California. The aircraft is pictured in June 1996 at Merced, California.

NC97651 was built in 1948 and spent all of its early life flying in and around Houston, Texas. When the first owner died in 1952, his wife kept the plane in storage until Cheney discovered it and bought it in 1991. He and his wife then spent three and a half years completely restoring it, including adding a beige leather interior by Debbie. The high standard of restoration of this aircraft has seen it win many awards at Fly-Ins throughout the Western U.S.

An improved version of the 1939 Model 105, Stinson introduced the Model 10 Voyager in April 1940. Production was terminated with America's entry into WW II, by which time, 760 Model 10s had been delivered.

The Model 108, which retained the Voyager name, was an enlarged post-war development of the Model 10. It was a four-seat, high-wing, cabin monoplane powered by a 165-hp Franklin 6A4-150-B3 engine and was built by the Stinson Division of Consolidated Vultee Aircraft Corp.

(Convair) alongside the lookalike Station Wagon utility model.

The 1945 post-war prototype was registered NX87600. By December 1948, Convair decided that Voyager production didn't fit its commercial and military production programme and sold the production rights to Piper Aircraft Corp. Piper phased out Voyager production in 1950 in favour of its own PA-20 Pacer. The Stinson 108 type certificate was subsequently acquired by Univair.

A total of 5,260 Model 108s were built, nearly 2,000 of which still survive.

A practical 4-seat tourer, the Station Wagon version was intended as a similar utility aircraft (GPJ).

Rescued from Texas in 1991, the Cheneys have restored their Voyager to *Concours* condition (GPJ).

Debbie Cheney was responsible for the leather cabin refurbishment (GPJ).

Dave Cheney flying his 1948 Stinson 108 Voyager (GPJ).

Above: Another fine US-based example of the Stinson 108 where the type is relatively common (GPJ).

Below: Rare British example of the Stinson 108, G-BHMR (ex F-BABO), at Middle Wallop, Hampshire in May 1982, one of many US classic aircraft imported to the UK in the 1980s by Cliff Lovell (GPJ).

Luscombe 11 Sedan (1948)

N1625B is owned by Ron Price based at Sonoma, California and was photo-graphed at Sonoma in May 1990 and air-to-air at Merced, California in June 1997.

Price bought the plane in 1983 from Oscar Schreiber in Canada after seeing an ad in *Trade-A-Plane*, America's leading aircraft-for-sale publication. He'd never flown a Sedan before, so Schreiber flew him across the Great Lakes to Detroit, giving him instruction along the way. By the time they landed, Price was ready to continue on his own, so Schreiber bid him farewell and returned home by ferry. Price continued on to Oshkosh, then took his new toy back home to California.

A Luscombe buff who also owns a rare Luscombe 4-90 (only four were ever built), Price has owned and flown it regularly ever since. He hangars it at his home field, Sonoma Sky Park in Northern California.

NX72402, the prototype Luscombe 11A Sedan, first flew in September 1946, powered by a 165-hp Continental E-165 engine. Post-war Luscombe production was in Dallas, Texas, where the Sedan was built alongside the more numerous and popular two-seat Luscombe 8F Silvaire. Production terminated in 1949 after 198 aircraft had been built, coinciding with the sale of the company to Temco Engineering, which was more interested in the Silvaire.

The Sedan was of all-metal construction, with a strut-braced high wing. The type certificate was sold and in 1970, Alpha Aviation Co. of Greenville, Texas who redesigned the Sedan as the Alpha IID, featuring a swept tail and tricycle gear. Alas, no aircraft were built and the type certificate passed to Classic Air of Lansing, Michigan.

In 1997, it was purchased by Oklahoma-based Luscombe Aircraft, which has announced plans to built its own version of the Alpha IID: the Spartan 185. Claiming a worldwide order book for 300 aircraft, the company plans to manufacture the type under licence in Australia, Brazil and the Netherlands.

A four-seater, only 198 Sedans were built – the type may yet be built again as the Spartan 185 (GPJ).

Above: Ron Price (left-hand seat) and fellow Luscombe fanatic Dwayne Green arrive at Sonoma Air Park, California in Ron's Luscombe 11 Sedan (GPJ).

Below: Not nearly as successful as the two-seat Luscombe 8, the Luscombe 11 Sedan (GPJ).

Ron Price acquired this Luscombe 11 Sedan in 1983 in Canada (GPJ).

Above: The strutted, high-wing configuration is clearly seen as Ron Price's Sedan departs (GPJ).

Below: One of over 100 Luscombe 8s, an 8E Silvaire, imported to the UK (this one in 1989), G-BRRB still sports its former US 'N-number' on the tail, N71184 (GPJ).

Cessna 170 (1955)

Finished in a factory scheme of red on polished bare metal, Ron Attig's Cessna 170B looks as good as the day it rolled off the production line in Wichita, Kansas 43 years ago. That wasn't always the case for the pampered Cessna based at Gillespie Field in San Diego, California.

When he first saw N4316B sitting in a hangar in Dwight, Illinois back in May 1990, 'It was in awful shape', Attig recalls. He got it ferryable, but had to fly it home with the windows open because of the stench of dead bugs and animals inside. Back in San Diego, Attig immediately gutted the plane and spent a year reconditioning it.

Although the plane's restoration to its present level of near-perfection was complete in 1993, the metal polishing is a chore that never ends. To help keep it to a minimum, though, Attig keeps N4316B under wraps in a set of snap-on covers custom-made for the plane by a friend.

'Restored 170s are appreciating at a rate of about $5,000 a year, so mine is now valued somewhere in the $35,000-$40,000 range', said Attig.

When sales of the two-seat Model 120/140 series began to flatten out, Cessna engineers enlarged the basic design to four places and called it the Model 170. Cessna was already producing the speedy, radial-engine 190/195 for the high-end executive market, so it pitched the 170 to the mid-level 'family' market.

The prototype first flew in September 1947 and production began the following spring. With its good looks, simple yet rugged design and rock-bottom $5,500 price tag, the 170 was an instant success. In the first year of production, Cessna delivered 1,000 170s and made big plans for the future.

For the 170A of 1949, they increased fuel capacity, replaced the fabric-covered wing with an all-metal one and the double strut with a single one and still managed to keep the list price under $6,000. Sales soared and in only four years, 2,250 170/170As had been delivered. That success inspired the

Model 170B, which debuted in early 1952.

With the addition of a number of minor changes, including larger, four-position flaps and a six-cylinder, 145-hp Continental O-300 engine, the 170B also sold like hotcakes. During its five-year production run, nearly 3,000 of them were built.

Attig's C-170B has traveled a long, winding road to its current stock configuration. The year after it was built, its owner groundlooped it and, inspired by the debut of the C-172 in November 1955, converted it to tricycle gear. He later landed it in a field and tore off the nose gear; when it was repaired a second time, it was converted back to a taildragger.

N4316B has approximately 1,800 hours on it to date, an average of 42 hours a year over 43 years. Attig says he's thoroughly enjoyed the time he's put on the plane, despite it being slightly underpowered.

Although it takes hours of buffing and polishing, owner Ron Attig prefers to keep his 1955 Cessna 170B in bare-metal rather than paint it (CRS).

Many of the civil Cessnas, as well as the military L-19 Bird Dog, evolved from the classic shape of the model 170B (CRS).

C-170's circular tail is identical in shape to the L-19's (CRS).

Retired structural iron worker Ron Attig bought this C-170 as a 'fixer-upper' and spent three years restoring it to its original glory (CRS).

Cessna 172 (1956)

Jim Landers bases his highly-polished straight-tail Cessna 172 at Falcon Field in Mesa, Arizona. Though it was in rough shape when he got it, it was still a good candidate for restoration.

N7252A (s/n 29352) rolled off the Wichita production line in late 1956. The original production flight-test report indicates the plane made its first flight on 20 December, 1956. During the 1960s, it spent time in Oneida, New York and Corpus Christi, Texas before ending up at Ryan Field outside Tucson, Arizona. It had three more owners before Landers bought it in 1992. Since then, he has put more than 600 hours on it, bringing the total airframe and engine times up to 3,900 and 1,600 hours, respectively.

Just before Cessna halted production of its entire line of single-engine light aircraft in 1986, the 172 passed the Me-109 fighter as the most prolific aircraft in history. During a 31-year production run, some 36,010 172s were built. And now that production has begun again, the numbers keep getting bigger.

The Cessna 172, which debuted in November 1955, wasn't an entirely new design, as it shared airframe components and dimensions with several earlier models. In fact, the prototype for all of Cessna's postwar four-seaters was the C-170, also featured in this book.

A year before the 172 took to the air, Obed Wells, project engineer on the 170/180, worked on his off-time to design and build a mockup of the Model 170 with a nosewheel instead of a tailwheel. Worried that a change to one of Cessna's most popular designs might harm sales, the company sales manager ordered the mockup destroyed. But because Wells thought he was onto something, he disassembled the mockup and put it in storage.

In 1955, Piper put a nosewheel on its four-place PA-20 Pacer and created the PA-22 Tri-Pacer, which was an instant hit with the flying public. With a nosewheel, flying (or at least landing and ground handling) suddenly became a lot easier and more popular. So it was the soaring sales of the Tri-Pacer, Beech Bonanza and Mooney Mark 20 that prompted Cessna management to resurrect Wells' mockup. Convinced it had to get on the nosewheel bandwagon or be left behind, Cessna immediately began development of the Model 172.

It, too, was an instant success, thanks to such features as doors on both sides, steering wheel-like control yokes rather than sticks and the 'Land-O-Matic' landing gear, a tricycle version of the innovative spring-steel gear Cessna introduced in 1946 on the Cessna 120. Cessna sold 1,178 172s at $8,750 each its first year on the market – 10 times the number of taildragger 170Bs sold that year.

The 170 had been Cessna's bread-and-butter airplane since 1948, but prompted by the overwhelming success of the 172, Cessna dropped the 170 line in 1956 in order to concentrate on the tricycle-gear 172, 'the plane of the future'.

Another fan of bare-metal finishes is Jim Landers of Mesa, Arizona, whose 1956 Cessna 172 is a shining example of what tender loving care can do for an aeroplane (CRS).

Like every Cessna 172 since, this straight-tail 1956 model is a comfortable easy-to-fly aeroplane, ideal as a family plane or flight trainer (CRS).

Reflection of the dual Venturi tubes on Landers' C-172 illustrates what is meant by the phrase 'mirror-finish' (CRS).

Though oldtimers thought Cessna ruined aviation by putting a nosewheel on the 172, it became one of Cessna's most popular designs, re-entering production in 1998 after a 12-year layoff (CRS).

The 172's 36-foot wingspan had an area of 175 square feet, which gave it very stable and gracious handling in the air (CRS).

Early 172s were powered by 145-hp Continental O-300A engines, which gave them a cruise speed of about 115-120 mph (CRS)

Cessna 150 (1959)

Some men never forget their first love and so it was with 79-year-old Vernon 'Andy' Andersen and the Cessna 150. He learned to fly in a straight-tail 150 at Flabob Airport in Rubidoux, California, so when it came time to buy his first airplane, he chose a 150.

It took three tries till he finally settled on this 1959 example, which he bought for $10,000 and spent several years bringing back to like-new condition.

N5641E has 3,315 hours on it, not bad for a 40-year-old trainer. Andersen is only the plane's fourth owner and put 550 of those hours (an average of 110 hours a year) on it.

'It flies just like every other 150', says Andersen of his pride and joy.

Introduced in late 1958 as a 1959 model, the C-150 was the plane Cessna used to re-enter the two-place market. It was basically a much updated follow-on to the successful Model 140 taildragger, which had been out of production for eight years. Priced at only $6,995 and powered by the reliable 100-hp Continental O-200-A, which gave it a cruise speed of 107 mph, the C-150 caught on quickly.

Rather than tamper with a success, Cessna produced the 150 virtually unchanged until 1966, when they gave it a slanted rather than a straight tail. Except for the introduction of the aerobatic 150K Aerobat in 1970, the 'Commuter' continued in production with only minor cosmetic changes through to the Model 150M in 1977.

In 1978, it was re-engined with a 110-hp Lycoming O-235 and renamed the Cessna 152. By then the most popular basic trainer in the world, production of the 150/152 continued until 1985. A total of 28,942 Model 150/152s were built, putting it in second place behind the 172 as Cessna's biggest seller.

To complement its four-place 172, Cessna introduced the two-place C-150 Commuter in 1958-59; it went on to become Cessna's most prolific trainer (CRS).

In recent years, the once overlooked Cessna trainer series are being purchased and restored by individual owners who give them the TLC flight schools never did (CRS).

Owner Andy Andersen, a 79-year-old retiree, uses his 150 mainly to visit friends and have lunch at local Southern California airports (CRS).

The owner, 79-year-old Andy Andersen, flies his 150 over Lake Matthews, a favourite Southern California photo location near his home base, Flabob Aiport (CRS).

Howard 500 (1963)

N500HP is owned by Rick Bourn and flown from Flying Cloud Airport in Minneapolis, Minnesota, where it was photographed in June 1998. Bourn, owner of Bourn Information Services, Inc., bought the Howard in December 1997 from Bruce Stevenson and his North Pacific Management Corp. in Portland, Oregon. Stevenson and his chief pilot, Dave Cummings, restored the plane in 1996-97; their workmanship was rewarded at Oshkosh '97 when the plane was named a 'Contemporary Grand Champion'.

N500HP's history is somewhat vague, but during the early 1970s, it was registered to Bohemia Oaks, Inc., the speculation being that it was one of Elvis Presley's companies.

A total of 22 Howard 500s were built in Texas between 1959 and 1964 and only two remain in airworthy condition: N500HP and Duncan Baker's N500LN, which is based but rarely flown at Exeter, England. The 500 is named after Durrell Unger 'Dee' Howard, who established an aircraft and engine maintenance and repair business in San Antonio, Texas that converted ex-WW II aircraft, particularly Lockheed Venturas and Harpoons, for use as corporate transports.

Although it resembles the Lockheed Harpoon, the Howard 500 was a completely new design, pressurised and capable of flying across the U.S. nonstop at an altitude of 25,000 feet. Unfortunately, it was up against Grumman's new, state-of-the-art Gulfstream I turboprop corporate transport. Even though its two Pratt & Whitney R-2800 radials made the Howard 500 a match for the Gulfstream in terms of performance, climb and range, it belonged to the WW II generation.

First flight of the Howard 500 was in March 1960, but certification delays until 1963 weakened its chance of success against the G-I.

Competitor to the Gulfstream 1 executive aircraft, only 22 Howard 500s were built (GPJ).

The Howard 500 taxying for take-off at Flying Cloud Airport, Minneapolis, Minnesota (GPJ).

Only two Howard 500s are believed to be left in airworthy condition in 1999 (GPJ).

Rick Bourn now owns and flies this unique Howard 500, assisted by his pilot Dave Cummings who has been with the aircraft through several recent owners (GPJ).

Piper PA-24 Comanche (1969)

N9469P (s/n 24-4979) is a Comanche 260C that was rebuilt and painted in Los Angeles in 1988 and ferried to Great Britain in 1991. Based at Guernsey, Channel Islands, it was flown over the Cherbourg Peninsula for these photos by Yvonne Burford, now a BAe-146 pilot for Jersey European Airways.

The prototype PA-24 made its first flight in May 1956, powered by a 180-hp Lycoming O-360-A1A engine. With its low-wing, four seats, retractable gear and all-metal construction, it was a revolutionary design step for Piper, whose previous single-engine offering had been the PA-22 Tri-Pacer.

The first certificated Comanche was delivered in June 1957. Powered by engines ranging from 180 to 400 hp, a total of 4,865 aircraft were built between 1956 and 1972.

Although this example was built in 1971, the first Comanche flew in 1956. N9469P spent many years flying in California before being imported to the UK in 1991 (GPJ).

Above: Unique quartet formation over Guernsey in September 1990 of three PA-24 Comanches and a PA-39 Twin Comanche (GPJ).

Below: Fully airways and IFR equipped cockpit of Comanche 260C N9469P – compare with those spartan, earlier cockpits depicted earlier in this book (GPJ).

APPENDIX: ANTIQUE & CLASSIC TYPE CLUBS

Aeronca Aviators Club: Joe Dickey, 55 Oakey Ave., Lawrenceburg, IN 47025; telephone 812/537-9354; e-mail: jdickey@seidata.com.

Aeronca Sedan Club: 115 Wendy Ct., Union Vity, CA 94587; telephone 510/487-3070.

American Bonanza Society: Nancy Johnson, P.O. Box 12888, Wichita, KS 67277; telephone 316/945-1700, fax 316/945-1710; website: www.bonanza.org.

American Navion Society: Jerry Feather, 59A Houston Lane, Lodi, CA 95240; telephone 209/339-4213, fax 209/339-1701.

American Yankee Association: P.O. Box 1531, Cameron Park, CA 95682; telephone 916/676-4292.

Antique Airplane Association: Robert L. Taylor, P.O. Box 127, Blakesburg, IA 52536; telephone 515/938-2773; website: www.aaa-apm.org.

Bamboo Bomber Club: Jim Anderson, Box 269, Sunwood, Marine on St Croix, MN 55047.

Bellanca-Champion Club: P.O. Box 708, Brookfield, WI 53008; telephone 414/784-4544.

Bird Airplane Club: Jeannie Hill, P.O. Box 328, Harvard, IL 60033; telephone 815/943-7205.

Buckeye Pietenpol Association: Grant MacLaren, 7 Crosswinds, St. Louis, MO 63132; telephone 314/677-1669 or 314/569-2846; e-mail: gmaclaren@ aol.com.

Cessna 150/152 Club: Skip Carden, P.O. Box 15388, Durham, NC 27704; telephone 919/471-9492, fax 919/477-2194.

Cessna 172/182 Club: Scott Jones, Wiley Post Airport, P.O. Box 22631, Oklahoma City, OK 73123; telephone 405/495-8664, fax 405/495-8666; website: www.cessna172-182club.com.

Cessna 310 Owners of America: 8531 Wealthwood, New Haven, IN 46774; telephone 219/749-2520, fax 219/749-6140.

Cessna Airmaster Club: Robert Taylor, Route 2, Box 172, Antique Airfield, Ottumwa, IA 52501.

Cessna Owners Organization: Bruce Loppnow, N-7450 Aanstad Rd., Iola, WI 54945; telephone 715/445-5000, fax 715/445-4053; website: www.aircraftownergroup.com.

Cessna Pilots Association: P.O. Box 12948, Wichita, KS 67277; telephone 800/852-2272 or 316/946-4777. Technical & Educational Facility, P.O. Box 5817, Santa Maria, CA 93456; telephone 805/922-2580, fax 805/922-7249; website: www.cessna.org.

Cherokee Pilots Association: Terry Rogers, P.O. Box 1996, Lutz, FL 33548; telephone 813/948-3616; website: www.piperowner.com.

Classic Jet Aircraft Association: Don Kirlin, Quincy Municipal Airport, Highway 104, Quincy, IL 62301; telephone 217/228-2522, fax 217/221-9999; e-mail: Don@Freefall.com.

Continental Luscombe Association: Loren Bump, 705 Riggs, Emmett, ID 83617.

Cub Club: John Bergeson, 6438 W. Millbrook, Remus, MI 49340; telephone 517/561-2393, fax 517/561-5101.

Culver Club: Larry Low, 60 Skywood Way, Woodside, CA 94062; telephone 650/851-0204.

Curtiss Robin Preservation Society: Robin's Nest, Jim Haynes, 21 Sunset Lane, Bushnell, IL 61422; telephone 309/772-2067; e-mail: robinnst@bushnell.net.

Dart Club: Lloyd Washburn, 2656 E. Sand Road, Port Clinton, OH 43452; telephone 419/734-6685.

Early Birds of Aviation: Neil Fisher, 267 DeHaven Rd., Beaver Falls, PA 15010; telephone 412/843-4504.

Eastern Cessna 190/195 Association: Cliff Crabs, 25575 Butternut Ridge Rd., North Olmsted, OH 44070; telephone 440/777-4025; e-mail: ccrabs@aol.com.

Ercoupe Owners Club: 3557 Roxboro Rd., Box 15388, Durham, NC 27704; telephone 919/471-9492.

Experimental Aircraft Association: Tom Poberezny, President, EAA Aviation Center, P.O. Box 3086, Oshkosh, WI 54903; telephone 920/426-4800, fax 920/426-4828; website: www.eea.org.

EAA Antique/Classic Division: EAA Aviation Center, P.O. Box 3086, Oshkosh, WI 54903; telephone 920/426-4800, fax 920/426-4828; website: www.antiqueclassic.org.

Fairchild Club: John W. Berendt, 7645 Echo Point Rd., Cannon Falls, MN 55009; telephone 507/263-2414, fax 507/263-0152.

Fairchild Fan Club: Robert L. Taylor, P.O. Box 127, Blakesburg, IA 52536; telephone ; website: www.aaa-apm.org.

Flying Apache Association: John Lumley, 6778 Skyline Dr., Delray Beach, FL 33446; telephone 561/499-1115, fax 561/495-7311; e-mail: jckl@compuserve.com.

Great Lakes Club: Brent Taylor, P.O. Box 127, Blakesburg, IA 52536; telephone 515/938-2773; website: www.aaa-apm.org.

Heath Parasol Club: William Schlapman; 6431 Paulson Rd., Winneconne, WI 54986; telephone 920/582-4454.

International 195 Club: Dwight Ewing, P.O. Box 737, Merced, CA 95340; telephone 209/722-6283, fax 209/722-5124.

International Aeronca Association: Buzz Wagner, P.O. Box 3, 401 1st Street East, Clark, SD 57225; telephone 605/532-3862.

International Cessna 120/140 Association: Bill Rhoades, 6425 Hazelwood Ave., Northfield, MN 55057; telephone 612/652-2221, fax 507/663-0098; e-mail: pilot140@aol.com.

International Cessna 170 Association: Velvet Fackeldey, P.O. Box 1667, Lebanon, MO 65536; telephone 417/532-4847.

International Cessna 180/185 Club: P.O. Box 222, Lebanon, MO 65536; telephone 417/532-4847.

International Challenger Owners Association: James George, 4817 Lovers Lane, Wichita Falls, TX 76310; telephone 940/696-2065.

International Comanche Society: P.O. Box 400, Grant, NE 69140; telephone 308/352-4275.

International Pietenpol Association: Robert L. Taylor, P.O. Box 127, Blakesburg, IA 52536; telephone 515/938-2773; website: www.aaa-apm.org.

International Swift Association: P.O. Box 644, Athens, TN 37303; telephone 615/745-9547.

International Taylorcraft Owners Club: Bruce Bixier, 12809 Greenbower Rd., Alliance, OH 44601; telephone 216/823-9748.

International Waco Magazine: P.O. Box 665, Destin, FL 32540; telephone 850/654-4205.

The Interstate Club: Robert L. Taylor, P.O. Box 127, Blakesburg, IA 52536; telephone 515/938-2773; website: www.aaa-apm.org.

Luscombe Association: John Bergeson, 6438 West Millbrook, Remus, MI 49340; telephone 517/561-2393, fax 517/561-5101.

Luscombe Foundation/The Don Luscombe Aviation History Foundation: Doug Combs, P.O. Box 63581, Phoenix, AZ 85082; telephone 602/917-0969, fax 602/917-4719; e-mail: silvair@luscombe.org. website: www.luscombe.org.

Meyers Aircraft Owners Association: Vinson Vanderford, 5852 Bogue Rd., Yuba City, CA 95993; telephone 530/673-2724.

Monocoupe Association: Bob Coolbaugh, 6154 River Forest Dr., Manassas, VA 22111.

Mooney Aircraft Pilots Association: Tom Canavera, P.O. Box 460607, San Antonio, TX 78246; telephone 210/525-8008, fax 210/525-8085; website: www.mooneyapa.com.

National Aeronca Association: 806 Lockport Rd., P.O. Box 2219, Terre Haute, IN 47802; telephone 812/232-1491.

National Biplane Association: Charles Harris, P.O. Box 470350, Tulsa, OK 74147; telephone 918/622-8400, fax 918/665-0039; e-mail: cwh@hvsu.com.

National Ryan Club: Bill Hodges, 19 Stoneybrook Lane, Searcy, AR 72143; telephone 501/268-2620, fax 501/279-4217; e-mail: bhodges@harding.edu.

National Stinson Club: Jonsey Paul, 14418 Skinner Rd., Cypress, TX 77429; telephone 281/373-0418.

National Stinson Club: Bill Snavely, 115 Heinley Rd., Lake Placid, FL 33852; telephone 941/465-6101; e-mail: stinsonioa@juno.com.

Northeast Stinson Flying Club: 8 Grimes Brook Rd., Simsbury, CT 06070; telephone 203/658-1566.

Piper Owners Society: Bruce Loppnow, N-7450 Aanstad Road, Iola, WI 54945; telephone 715/445-5000, fax 715/445-4053; website: www.aircraftownergroup.com.

Porterfield Airplane Club: Chuck Lebrecht; 91 Hickory Loop, Ocala, FL 34472; telephone 352/687-4859.

Rearwin Club: Robert L. Taylor, P.O. Box 127, Blakesburg, IA 52536; telephone 515/938-2773; website: www.aaa-apm.org.

Seabee Club International: 6761 N.W. 32nd Ave., Ft. Lauderdale, FL 33309; telephone 305/979-5470.

Short-Wing Piper Club: Eleanor Mills, 220 Main, P.O. Box 71, Halstead, KS 67056; telephone 316/835-2235, fax 316/835-3357; website: www.shortwing.com.

Southwest Stinson Club: Dennis Dow, 3005 6th St., Sacramento, CA 95818; telephone 916/446-3729; e-mail: ddow@aeromar.com.

Staggerwing Club: Jim Gorman, 1885 Millsboro Rd., Mansfield, OH 44906; telephone 419/529-3822 (home), 419/755-1223 (office), fax 419/755-1233.

Stearman Restorers Association: Brian Riggs, 3913 Red Leaf Ct., Point of Rocks, MD 21777; telephone 301/874-0923.

Straight-Tail Cessna Club: Lee Cornett, 2 Forest Lane, Gales Ferry, CT 06335; telephone 860/464-7044.

Super Cub Pilots Association: Jim Richmond, P.O. Box 9823, Yakima, WA 98909; telephone 509/248-9491, fax 509/248-1421; website: www.cubcrafters.com.

Swift Museum Foundation: Charles Nelson, McMinn County Airport, Hangar 4, P.O. Box 644, Athens, TN 37303; telephone 423/745-9547, fax 423/745-9869.

Taylorcraft Owners Club: 12809 Greenbower Rd., Alliance, OH 44601; telephone 216/823-9748.

Travel Air Club: Robert L. Taylor, P.O. Box 127, Blakesburg, IA 52536; telephone 515/938-2773; website: www.aaa-apm.org.

Twin Beech Association: Enrico Bottieri, P.O. Box 8186, Fountain Valley, CA 92728; telephone 714/964-4864; e-mail: 71061.1225@compuserve.com.

Twin Bonanza Association: Richard Ward, 19684 Lakeshore Dr., Three Rivers, MI 49093; telephone 616/279-2540; e-mail: forward@net.link.net.

The Twin Cessna Flyer: Larry Ball, 512 Broadway, Ste. 102, New Haven, IN 46774; telephone 219/749-2520, 800/825-5310, fax 219/749-6140; e-mail: Twinces@aol.com.

Vintage Sailplane Association: George Nuse, 4310 River Bottom Dr., Norcross, GA 30092; telephone 770/446-5533.

Waco Historical Society: William F. Laufer, 105 South Market St., P.O. Box 62, Troy, OH 45373; telephone 937/335-1742, fax 937/335-9647.

West Coast Cessna 120.140 Club: P.O. Box 727, Rosebud, OR 97470; telephone 503/459-5103.

World Beechcraft Society: Alden C. Barrios, 1436 Muirlands Dr., La Jolla, CA 92037; telephone 619/565-9735, fax 619/459-2745.